17 Days That Changed America

By

Dr. Michael F. Price

Deep Indigo Books

Published by Indigo Sea Press
Winston-Salem

Deep Indigo Books
Indigo Sea Press
302 Ricks Drive
Winston-Salem, NC 27103

This book is a work of non-fiction as faithfully recreated by the author. All events, individuals, dates and settings are solely part of the author's process and recollection.

First Deep Indigo Books edition published
August 2022
Deep Indigo Books, Moon Sailor and all production design are trademarks of Indigo Sea Press, used under license.

For information regarding bulk purchases of this book, digital purchase and special discounts, please contact the publisher at indigoseapress@gmail.com

Cover photo provided courtesy of
the Point Pleasant River Museum
Manufactured in the United States of America
ISBN 978-1-63066-543-2

With Gratitude

There is a common belief that getting a book from the hands of its author into the hands of the public is a singular effort. Nothing could be further from the truth. Such a feat requires a symphony of skilled individuals, each performing their skills behind the scenes. Yes, ask anyone who has ever had anything published, and if they're honest, they'll tell you there are many names behind the name on the book's cover. This work is no exception.

My sincere gratitude goes out to all those that assisted me over the past eleven months to get this work to its completion. I couldn't have done it without you.

For starters, there are those longtime Point Pleasant residents like Sandy Dunn, John Musgrave, and Stephen Littlepage. They took time from their busy schedules during several cold days in late winter to meet and talk. Their valuable insights and vivid memory of the events on both sides of the Ohio River following the collapse of the Silver Bridge provided me with a solid foundation on which to build. The same applies to individuals like Judy (Chapman) Kirtland, Shirley (Chapman) Kurz, and retired Coast Guard member Joe Mason. All three provided me with priceless context and first-person insight into the events before, during, and after that horrific December 1967 tragedy. Kirtland was on the bridge when it collapsed and survived to tell about it. Her sister, Shirley, was volunteering at Holzer Hospital the night of the collapse. As for Mason, he was part of a Coast Guard crew charged with transporting lifeless bodies from the river to waiting ambulances.

Then there was Chris Rizer, whose role as president of the Mason County Historical and Preservation Society, Executive Director of Main Street Point Pleasant, and regular contributor to the *Point Pleasant Register*, provided me with the historical perspective so crucial in a work such as this. And when I needed a critical piece of information, Miranda Rousch in the Mason County Clerk's Office, Aimee Duncan with the Mason County Tax Assessor's office, and Kaitlynn Halley, Assistant Director, Gallia County Convention and Visitors Bureau, came to the rescue. Finally, my deep gratitude goes to Beaufort County, North Carolina, resident Loretta Blanks. She not only put me in contact with Joe Mason but was willing to share her top-notch research skills and insights.

Equally valuable in this whole process of getting my book published were those that proofread the work. A hearty thank you goes out to Debbie Miller and Bill Northrup. With a deep commitment and enduring patience, they offered their precious time to read through the book, grammatical errors and all, and provide insights into making the work more meaningful. These two individuals are diamonds in the rough.

The same appreciation is extended to my breakfast buddies, Jay Miller and Linda Grauer. Their listening ears and caring hearts allowed me to ramble about bridge construction and eyebars even at 8:00am on Sunday mornings. I guess that's one of the benefits of friendship.

The Chichester Court Bed and Breakfast owners in Raleigh, North Carolina, also deserve thanks. Proprietors, Brad and Hannah, made my visits to the area refreshing and energizing. Moreover, the cost for "three hots and a cot" was perfect for my limited budget. As for the young staff of the B&B, including Nabby, Muffin, and Pepper, their animated conversation and astute observations stirred my soul…morning, noon, and night.

Once more, my sincerest gratitude goes to Dr. Mike Simpson and the good folks at Indigo Sea Press in Kernersville, North Carolina. This makes the fifth time that I have worked with Mike and his staff to have a book published. Each time, they displayed unlimited patience, provided impeccable insights, and showed outstanding professionalism throughout the process. Words cannot express my sincere thanks.

Finally, my deepest gratitude goes out to my wife, Betty.

Despite her declining health and absence of memory, being in her presence reminded me that life is more than books about bridges. Although the physical pages of this book will fade over time, her companionship, encouragement, and emotional support over the years will remain. Thank you, Lovey. You have made me a better husband, father, and human being.

—Dr. Michael F. Price

Table of Contents

The Introduction

"Where were you when you first heard about it?" It's a common question that's been asked countless times over the years.

For me, it was Saturday morning, December 16, 1967, not long after 8:00am. I had just finished my newspaper route and had returned home to the warmth of our house on Maple Avenue. As I handed my mother her copy of the *Wheeling Intelligencer* and began reading, she sighed. "There was a bridge collapse last night down near Huntington," she says, "and a lot of people have died."

At the time, the news meant little to me. My thoughts were more on what I might be receiving for Christmas, my 13th birthday in less than a month, listening to the latest music by The Monkees, or trying to convince my mother to allow me to go to the Lincoln Theater downtown to watch Dustin Hoffman in The Graduate when it comes out later in the month. Nearly a half-century later, something happened recently, somewhat serendipitously, that reminded me of that tragic event that claimed forty-six lives, left several families on both sides of the Ohio River devastated, and temporarily separated two communities that had been made one by a bridge built just before the Depression.

I had no sooner finished reading David McCullough's masterpiece on the Brooklyn Bridge than I received an envelope from my oldest brother, Frank. On occasion, he has been known to send me things that he thinks I might enjoy, like a cartoon, a short newspaper article, or a bit of sports trivia. This time, however, there was only one thing in the envelope...an article on the collapse of the Silver Bridge that took place on Friday evening, December 15, 1967, in Point Pleasant, West Virginia. The convergence of these two events, McCullough's book and Frank's mailing, sent me on a journey to write this book.

Granted, other books have been written over the past fifty-five years, and each has contributed to a general understanding of the bridge's collapse. The last one published was in 2015. Before that, there was a work published a decade ago, and it

6

greatly aided the public's knowledge of events surrounding the tragedy through the medium of photographs. Still, I felt it was time that someone took a closer, more comprehensive look at the bridge's history, the events before, during, and after the collapse, and add depth and detail. It was time that someone took a closer look… month by month, week by week, day by day, even hour by hour…at what really took place during those *17 Days That Changed America*. The time is calling for someone to combine these various stories and form them into one narrative.

My initial path was to take a professional look at when and why the bridge was built and trace how the bridge became such a vital economic and social lifeline between Point Pleasant and Gallipolis, Ohio. Moreover, it was my goal to write a book that was objective, unbiased, and, most of all, original. However, the more I researched, the more the story became personal. Those who died were fathers and mothers with young children. They were teachers and students, veterans that had served our country honorably, retirees, truck drivers, and everyday workers that made our lives comfortable. And when I thought about how the lives of these forty-six people came to a sudden end, I thought about the times when I, as a minister, had to go to a home and tell a family that one of their loved ones has died or when I had to give the eulogy at the funeral for a teenager. The work went from being professional to personal and then to pastoral when I read about how a nine-month pregnant, Glenna Taylor, told her parents that this Christmas would be the best ever, of Kathy Byus' grandmother having to collect her granddaughter's belongings from school, and the excruciating pain of reading that two bodies were never found.

I am fully convinced that my past has prepared me for such an endeavor as writing this book. My undergraduate years at West Liberty State College, now a university, instilled in me a love of history, and my time as a graduate student at West Virginia University taught me how to research, as did my seminary years at Brite Divinity School, Texas Christian University. And finally, it was during my five years as a doctoral candidate that I learned to write. This said, I'll let you be the judge when you finish reading this book if I'm qualified to write such a story.

As expected, questions will arise as to my sources. It's natural when one writes anything historical. I was limited in getting interviews with survivors because most have passed away. The last of the nine survivors plucked from the Ohio River and escaped death on the night of the collapse died in 2021. While most of the children of the survivors are too young to remember, those in their 20s and 30s at the time of the collapse are now in their late 70s and beyond. Subsequently, my primary source became national, state, and local newspapers, with the website *newspaperarchive.com* as my starting point. This allowed me to compare and contrast articles. It did not take long for me to decipher which articles were factual and which included some untruths, which were written to entertain rather than inform, which pieces were "off the wire," and which were written by writers who were actually on the scene. One misspelled name, one incorrect line about the number of fatalities, or one false statement about this or that, and it was too late to make corrections once the story hit national circulation. In all cases, I proceeded with caution to get the facts correct. When there is a discrepancy in the spelling of a person's name (e.g., Blackmon and Blackman, Cremeans and Cremeens, Herd and Head, Simms and Sims, Marjorie for Margaret, Kristy and Christy, Forrest and Forest, etc.), I change the spelling to how the name appears on the person's tombstone or grave marker according to *findagrave.com*. I do the same for other misspellings (e.g., Ashboro to Asheboro, etc.).

The most productive sources were the local and regional newspapers, including the *Athens* (Ohio) *Messenger*, *Charleston Daily Mail*, the *Charleston Gazette*, the *Gallipolis Daily Tribune,* the (Huntington, West Virginia) *Herald-Dispatch*, the *Herald-Advertiser*, and the *Point Pleasant Register*. Local and regional papers followed the story from beginning to end, from the pre-construction of the Silver

Bridge in the 1920s, its collapse in 1967, and the dedication of the new bridge in 1969. The local and regional newspapers not only shared with readers who were on the bridge when it fell but why they were on the bridge and where they were going to or coming from. These newspapers were invaluable because they provided details and told "the story behind the story." I relied heavily on the local newspapers because they offered local weather conditions and what was happening across the seas and across the street. Moreover, local reporters refused to let the story go away and die. Best of all, the newspapers that printed both a morning and an afternoon edition allowed any last-minute details to get to the readers.

Two other sources were equally valuable, including the 151-page, *After Action Report of the Corps. of Engineers*, issued in March 1968, and the final report of the *National Transportation Safety Board of the Silver Bridge Collapse*, published on October 31, 1968. Last but not least, it goes without saying that David McCullough's book on the Brooklyn Bridge helped tremendously by educating me about bridge construction and terms like cofferdams and caissons. My greatest joy was to put these stories from various sources into a chronological narrative.

And while we're on the subject of the book's contents, you must keep a few things in mind. First, I plead with you to read this book as if it's an unfolding and developing story, even though we all know how the story comes out. Try reading the book within its intended scope: the four decades or so between the mid-1920s and the late 1960s. Equally, it's important to remember that statistics are in a constant state of fluidness, and things are changing at the bridge site by the day, if not by the hour. Fifty years ago, there was no such thing as "real-time." Next, please remember that although the content of some of the chapters may decrease in size and volume, it has nothing to do with my waning interest in telling this story. Like any good historian, I allowed the facts to lead me.

As bridge-related articles became less and less over time and the stories slowly dried up, there was less and less to write about. Hopefully, this explains why I shifted from daily or weekly events in the early pages to monthly ones as the story went on. In like manner, you will notice very few citations among the pages. I did this mainly to keep the cost of the book as low as possible. Extra pages equal extra costs. Who knows how much the book would cost if I had included the numerous citations and references that proved so central to the story. Besides, I know very few who actually read the reference page! If you want to know where I located some particular piece of information found in the work, call or write me. I'll be glad to help.

Further, I tried as much as possible not to use too many names and describe personal details. Stuff like this only seems to dilute the story. While this runs contrary to newspaper articles at the time that mentions everything from who's traveling, who's in the hospital and why, and who's been called for jury duty, I respect privacy and honor confidentiality.

One last thing I ask that you remember: this work is not about the survivors. It's not about those who can thank their lucky stars they didn't make it on the bridge that night in December 1967. Getting caught by a red light, making an unplanned stop, or running late proved to be a blessing in disguise. They can tell their own story. Just ask them.

Instead, this book is about those that did not make it home that cold night over fifty years ago. It's about the scores of everyday people whose acts of compassion and caring came through when needed most and who stepped up when others stepped back during seventeen days between December 15 and 31. Above all else, this book is about people who showed up and gave their time and talent to help two communities torn apart by one horrific tragedy be made whole again, and how one bridge connecting two small towns taught America some valuable lessons.

The River

Called "the Good River" by the Seneca Indians, "La Belle Riviere" (The Beautiful River) by early French explorers, and "the River Jordan" by enslaved people seeking emancipation, my fellow West Virginians and our Ohio neighbors who were born and raised in towns along its path refer to it simply as "the river." And as one of this country's most traveled and majestic waterways, the sheer beauty of the Ohio River stands toe-to-toe with its illustrious past.

Formed by the confluence of the Allegheny River and the Monongahela River in downtown Pittsburgh, Pennsylvania, the river then flows north and west for approximately 40 miles toward Hancock County in northern West Virginia. The river turns and begins heading south in the far western part of the panhandle near Chester. And for nearly 250 miles, the Ohio River forms a natural boundary between West Virginia and its neighbor to the immediate west, the state of Ohio. It makes a westerly turn not far from Huntington, West Virginia, and continues its trek toward Cincinnati, Louisville, and points beyond. The river ends its nearly 1,000-mile journey at the Mississippi River near Cairo, Illinois. In the end, the river will have flowed through or bordered six states, including the Keystone State (Pennsylvania), the Mountain State (West Virginia), the Buckeye State (Ohio), the Bluegrass State (Kentucky), the Hoosier State (Indiana), and the Prairie State (Illinois). Despite its length, the Ohio River is by no means the longest river in the U.S. It's not even in the top ten rivers in size. Instead, the Ohio is number 11 in total length, just behind the Snake River and ahead of the Colorado River in Texas and the Tennessee River. For the record, the longest river in the U.S. is the Missouri River.

With no less than twenty-five tributaries in the tri-state area (Pennsylvania, Ohio, and West Virginia) supplying run-off to the Ohio River, it is no wonder why the river became so crucial for those who chose to live along its banks. Besides the donations provided by the Allegheny and Monongahela Rivers, four tributaries, one river, and three creeks join the Ohio River from Pennsylvania. Of the fourteen tributaries from Ohio, there are ten creeks and four rivers. The biggest river of these is the Muskingum River which empties into the Ohio at Marietta. As for West Virginia, ten creeks or rivers dump their water into the river. Of this number, eight are creeks, including Wheeling Creek in Ohio County, Fishing Creek near New Martinsville, and Middle Island Creek in Tyler County, and two are rivers. One of these rivers is the Kanawha River which joins the Ohio just south of Point Pleasant, West Virginia. As expected, these tributaries keep the Ohio River relatively "full" year-round. Meanwhile, the counties and towns on both sides of the river are familiar to Ohioans and West Virginians alike.

———————

One finds no less than ten counties on the eastern side of the river, the West Virginia side. Among these counties that run north to south along the river and comprise nearly one-fifth of the state's fifty-five counties are Hancock, Brooke, Ohio, Marshall, Wetzel, Tyler, Pleasants, Wood, Jackson, and Mason. The county seat of Mason County is the city of Point Pleasant. These counties were formed before West Virginia was granted statehood on June 20, 1863. Most interesting, one county on the list, Ohio County, became a county the same year this country declared its independence from England! And if one were to add Cabell County, situated to the south of Point Pleasant, to the count, there would be eleven West Virginia counties with shorelines along the Ohio River. Between the city of Chester in the north and Point Pleasant, located at the opposite end of these ten counties, are countless towns and cities dotting the banks of the river, including New Cumberland, Weirton, Wheeling, McMechen, Moundsville, New Martinsville, Paden City, Sistersville, St. Marys, Williamstown, Parkersburg, Ravenswood, and Mason.

A similar thing could be said for the state of Ohio. Of the eighty-eight counties that comprise the state, nearly one in ten lies within sight of the West Virginia shoreline. As some of the first counties settled when the Northwest Territory was officially opened in the latter years of the 18th century, it is little wonder why local leaders chose such respected names to call the counties of Columbiana (for Christopher Columbus), Washington, Jefferson, and Monroe (after presidents), Athens (for Athens, Greece), and Gallia (after the Gaul name for France since most of the early settlers in the area were of French descent). As for Belmont County, the name means "beautiful" in French, while Meigs County gets its name from one of the state's early governors, Return Meigs. Except for the two counties formed before 1800, Washington and Jefferson, the remaining six were created before 1819.

Conversely, except for Brooke, Ohio, and Wood counties formed in the last decade of the 1700s, the remaining West Virginia counties on the list were all created after 1830. Clearly, while the counties on the east side of the river may have been some of the last in the state to be formed, the counties located on the west side of the river, the Ohio side, may have been some of the first in that state. As for Ohio towns and cities located between East Liverpool (Columbiana County) in the north and Gallipolis (Gallia County), located just across the river from Point Pleasant in the south, one finds towns and cities on the west bank of the river with names such as Steubenville, Martins Ferry, Hannibal, Clarington, New Matamoras, Marietta, Belpre, Racine, and Pomeroy. Marietta holds the title of the first permanent settlement in the Northwest Territory.

In addition to its historical value in opening up new lands, the Ohio River has also been instrumental to the economy and commerce of West Virginia and its neighbor to the west, Ohio. The use of water transportation to move coal and other vital products up and down the river has long been commonplace. Though navigation may have been standard on the river, the use of the river to move things and people became widespread not long after the end of the Civil War, especially as the river took people and goods to the south and west.

Last but not least, the river was understood by freedom seekers as a symbolic dividing line between slavery and emancipation, in the same way that the Mason-Dixon Line was seen as a dividing line between north and south. Safely across the river and now in a free state like Ohio, those seeking freedom were given food, clothing, and safe shelter. Subsequently, those towns and cities on either side of the river, such as Gallia County, Ohio, or Mason County, West Virginia, became critical "stations" along the infamous Underground Railroad.

By the turn of the 20th century, two elements began to surface that greatly aided transportation and commerce. Moreover, each of these structural wonders benefitted people and businesses on both sides of the river.

The first of eight dams to be built on the river between Pittsburgh and Gallipolis is the Emsworth Dam. It is located 6 miles or so from Pittsburgh and went into operation in 1921. Less than 10 miles down the river from the Emsworth Dam and built less than a decade later, the Dashields Dam was completed in 1929. A third dam, the Montgomery Dam, was opened in 1936, and is located some 30 miles south of Pittsburgh near Monaca, Pennsylvania. Among the West Virginia dams is the New Cumberland Dam, which opened in 1961 and is approximately 25 miles south of the Montgomery Dam. The Pike Island Dam is located about 100 miles south of Pittsburgh and opened in the mid-1960s. The three remaining dams to the south include the Belleview Dam, placed in operation in 1965, the Racine Dam, which opened in 1967, and the Gallipolis Dam, built-in 1937 and located some 40 miles south of the Racine Dam. The last three dams are 200 miles, nearly 240 miles, and approximately 280 miles south of Pittsburgh. According to most calculations, the average distance between dams operating on the Ohio River is 20 to 30 miles. In addition to reducing the number of antiquated dams between Pittsburgh and Gallipolis, the effort also increased the river's depth in some spots to 25-30 feet. Consequently, the move allowed bigger boats to haul larger loads, which increased commercial navigation.

A second and equally rewarding effort came when bridges began being built that crossed the river. One of the first bridges built connecting West Virginia and Ohio was on the river's northern part.

The *Chester/Newell Toll Bridge*, connecting Chester/Newell, West Virginia, and East Liverpool, Ohio, was built by the American Bridge Company in 1905. Built as a suspension bridge and utilizing wire cables to hold the roadway, the structure has two one-way traffic lanes and offers a pedestrian walkway. While it remains one of the last suspension bridges over the river, it was initially constructed so workers living in East Liverpool could safely travel to the Homer Laughlin Pottery Factory in Chester.

Connecting Market Street in Steubenville, Ohio, with Route 2 in Follansbee, West Virginia, the *Market Street Bridge*, also known as the Steubenville Bridge, was constructed in 1905. At first, the bridge, which measures nearly 1,800 feet long and stands almost 70 feet above the river, was opened solely to foot traffic and charged a nickel fee to walk from one side to the other. The bridge's site foreman and his wife were the first to drive a vehicle over the span.

Built in 1928, the *Weirton-Ft. Steuben Bridge*, also known as the Ft. Steuben or Stanton Bridge, is a suspension bridge approximately one mile from the Market Street Bridge. With a total length of nearly 1,600 feet and a middle span of almost 700 feet, the bridge began as a toll bridge, but tolls were removed in 1953. Like the Newell Bridge to the north, the bridge handles two lanes of one-way traffic. The state's purchase of the bridge for around $1.3 million in 1941 meant that the bridge's care and maintenance were now in the hands of West Virginia.

Moving south along the river, the next bridge to cross the main channel of the Ohio River is the *Ft. Henry Bridge*. Built in 1955 and maintained by the state of West Virginia, the bridge is named after Patrick Henry and is a 4-lane road with two lanes in each direction. The total length of the span is approximately 1,660 feet, with the longest span about one-third of the bridge's entire length.

With a total span of over 2,700 feet, the *Bellaire Bridge* is a privately-owned toll bridge that connects Benwood, West Virginia, with Bellaire, Ohio. Designed by the J. E. Greiner Company and completed in 1926, the bridge stands over 350 feet above the river. Initial tolls were five cents for a one-way trip. On Independence Day 1927, a female from Wheeling and her groom from Bellaire exchanged marriage vows while on the span.

Approximately 35 miles south of the Bellaire Bridge is the *New Martinsville Bridge*, also known as the Korean Veterans Memorial Bridge. As a two-lane road with one-way traffic connecting Hannibal, Ohio, and New Martinsville, West Virginia, the bridge is over 2,000 feet long, with the longest span measuring nearly 725 feet. It opened in 1961.

Opened in 1928 and constructed using eyebar suspension, the *Hi Carpenter Bridge* has its east entrance located in St. Marys, West Virginia, in Pleasants County. The west end of the bridge is in Newport, Ohio. Named after local legend Hiram Carpenter, who did much to get the bridge built, the main span is over 700 feet long and was operated as a toll bridge. During the bridge's construction, part of the uncompleted span collapsed, and three men died. A fourth man from New Martinsville jumped off the bridge and into the swift waters below and drowned.

Traveling some twenty-two miles to the south of the Hi Carpenter Bridge, one finds the *Memorial Bridge*, connecting Belpre, Ohio, with Parkersburg, West Virginia. This tolled, three-span bridge, totaling nearly 2,600 feet in length, was completed in 1954 and is a two-lane road with one-way traffic.

Built in 1928, the *Mason-Pomeroy Bridge* connects Mason, West Virginia, and Pomeroy, Ohio. The bridge, a two-lane, nearly 1,850-foot span, sits almost 170 feet above the river, and is located along U.S. Highway 33.

The last of the ten bridges that solely span the Ohio River

between West Virginia and Ohio is the *Silver Bridge* which connects the cities of Point Pleasant, West Virginia, and Gallipolis, Ohio. It lies nearly fifteen miles downstream from the Mason-Pomeroy Bridge and almost fifty miles upstream from Sixth Street Bridge in Huntington. The width of the Ohio River at the bridge's location is nearly 1,250 feet.

The Silver Bridge has several similarities with its sister bridges to the north. As with the Newell Bridge, there is a pedestrian walkway on the Silver Bridge. Like the Market Street Bridge, the bridge supervisor of the Silver Bridge was the first to drive a vehicle across the bridge. Just like the Weirton-Ft. Steuben Bridge and the Ft. Henry Bridges, the maintenance of the Silver Bridge falls under the care of the state of West Virginia. The Bellaire Bridge and the Silver Bridge were designed by the J. E. Greiner Company. In addition, the New Martinsville Bridge, the Memorial Bridge in Parkersburg, and the Silver Bridge are two-lane roads. Finally, the Hi Carpenter Bridge and the Silver Bridge were constructed using eyebar suspension.

However, there is one tragic and glaring difference between the Silver Bridge and the other bridges. The other bridges didn't collapse!

The Bridge

The area's rich history is not lost on the two cities on opposite sides of the Ohio River. In their own way, each deserves a degree of attention even though they are straddled by the river.

Located on a "point" on the eastern shore of the Ohio River, the city of Point Pleasant lies north of the confluence of the Kanawha River and the Ohio. In 1749, the area was claimed by French explorer Céloron de Blainville, who buried a lead plaque at the confluence of the two rivers, naming the place Point Pleasant. Widely believed to be built on an old frontier fort, the city is the oldest settlement on the Ohio River south of Wheeling. Moreover, it is said that Point Pleasant is nearly three hundred and seventy days older than Wheeling and twelve years older than Charleston, West Virginia. Similarly, the city that sits on the eastern side of the Silver Bridge is believed to be fourteen years older than Marietta, fifteen years older than Cincinnati, and seventeen years older than Gallipolis. Point Pleasant is also thought to be nearly two decades older than the oldest town in Kentucky, the town of Harrodsburg. George Washington is reported to have surveyed the area and noted in his journal that the area would be an excellent location for a western capital. In 1774, a battle took place near the city and is believed to be the first of the American Revolution. Shortly before the end of the century (1794), the Virginia legislature officially recognized Point Pleasant as a town. A decade later, the area was carved out of nearby Kanawha County and became Mason County, named for American patriot and politician George Mason. The city of Point Pleasant was designated to be the county seat shortly after that. By the turn of the 20th century, the population had grown to approximately 2,000, and by the mid-1960s, the population had nearly tripled, thanks to a thriving downtown. Centrally located, the city of Point Pleasant is about 60 miles northwest of Charleston and 45 miles north of the state's second-largest city, Huntington. Parkersburg, the state's third-largest city, is located less than 60 miles north. Finally, the city sits on the heavily traveled Route 35, which begins west of

Charleston, continues toward Columbus, Ohio, and ends nearly 425 miles later in Michigan City, Indiana.

Gallipolis, termed by many as the "Best Known Small City in Ohio," is on the opposite side of the Ohio River and a few miles to the south of Point Pleasant. Organized in the late 1700s by approximately 500 French settlers who traveled south on the Ohio River from Pittsburgh, Gallipolis is one of the oldest cities in what is known as the Northwest Territory. However, Gallipolis is a "young" city compared to many others in the region. It is 14 years younger than Marietta, 15 years younger than Cincinnati, and nearly 20 years younger than Point Pleasant.

As Gallipolis grew over the years, the city not only became a noted regional port but was recognized for its high-quality boatbuilding. Early visitors include the French commander, the Marquis de Lafayette. It is believed that the first postmaster was a friend and schoolmate of Napoleon Bonaparte. By the turn of the 20th century, Gallipolis had grown to over 5,400 residents, and by the mid-1960s, the population was above 8,000. Beyond being the summer home of famous newspaper writer O. O. McIntyre, Gallipolis is also the site of the Ohio Hospital for Epileptics, the first hospital in America dedicated to caring for epileptics, and the home of Holzer Hospital, recognized at one time by the American College of Surgeons as one of the most modern and best-equipped hospitals in the state. While the north-south Route 7 runs through the city, drivers traveling west can pick up Route 35 in the unincorporated settlement of Kanauga north of the city. Columbus, Ohio, is a little over 100 miles to the north and west, while Cincinnati is due west, approximately 150 miles.

Beyond the river travel, the two cities had at their pleasure railroad lines. The B&O (Baltimore & Ohio) Railroad and the New York Central served the residents of Point Pleasant. Across the river, a branch of the C&O (Chesapeake & Ohio) served Gallipolis residents. In 1893, the K&M (Kanawha & Michigan) Railroad built a railroad bridge across the Ohio. The trestle lies several hundred yards north of Point Pleasant. No vehicle bridge directly connects the two cities. The nearest bridges are forty-five miles downstream in Huntington and over fifty miles upstream in Parkersburg.

In the latter years of the first decade of the 1900s, Dr. Charles Hamilton, a well-known surgeon, made a medical trip to southeastern Ohio to perform an operation. Hamilton was accompanied by a medical school resident named Charles E. Holzer. When asked about relocating to the area following his graduation, Holzer said that the area would be the last place in the world he would practice. Strikingly, following his graduation from medical school at the Ohio State University, Dr. Holzer takes a job at the Ohio Hospital for Epileptics at Gallipolis. His plan is to spend one year at the hospital to gain additional surgical experience. However, as the only surgeon in the area, it was not uncommon for Holzer to care for patients who were not residents of the hospital. When World War I broke out, he closed the hospital and joined the service as a second lieutenant. Upon returning, Holzer decides to stay in Gallipolis and sets up a practice. Recognizing the increasing medical needs of a growing community, he converts a house in Gallipolis into a multi-bed hospital. It was the only hospital within a 40-mile radius. Before long, the hospital is expanded to a 25-bed facility.

Six years later, the hospital not only expands to nearly triple patient capacity but installs air conditioning, making it one of the first in the state to have such a distinction. Before long, Dr. Holzer is tending to the medical needs of individuals across the river in West Virginia and patients in Ohio. To take care of the needs of his patients on the east side of the river usually requires him to take a rowboat or ferry across the Ohio from Gallipolis. The same stands true for those on the West Virginia side who travel to Dr. Holzer's office in Ohio. It is perilous during the winter months when ice could form on the river's banks or when the river overflows its banks in the spring. It is said that more than one of his patients died while waiting for Dr. Holzer to arrive. After one such episode, he decides that something must be done.

Around December 1925, it is believed Holzer introduces the idea of the need for a bridge to be built that would connect the two shores. Before long, a group is organized, calling itself the Gallia County Ohio Bridge Company. The group members begin approaching politicians at the federal level seeking congressional approval to construct a bridge across the river. The news catches on quickly and is well-received among people on both sides of the Ohio. Subsequently, several groups on the West Virginia side of the Ohio are working to complement the efforts on the opposite side of the river.

It is believed that sometime before March 1926, the Gallia County Ohio River Bridge Company was "…incorporated for the purpose of constructing a toll bridge across the Ohio River between Gallipolis, Ohio, and Point Pleasant, West Virginia." The articles of incorporation read:

> Gallipolis, Ohio, and Point Pleasant, West Virginia, are located on opposite banks of the Ohio River. In 1926 each community had an expanding population; each was a prosperous regional commercial center and growing industrial area; each had railroad service. Moreover, roads for automobile traffic running from the capital cities of Ohio and West Virginia to Gallipolis to Point Pleasant, respectively, had recently undergone or were then undergoing improvement. No bridge, however, directly connected the two towns; the nearest bridges were forty-two miles downstream and fifty-one miles upstream.

Beyond paying the $10,000 to incorporate, the list of members of the company includes Dr. Charles Holzer, president, Henry W. Cherrington, Dr. Leo Bean, Dr. J. T. Hanson, and J. E. Holliday.

Before long, two bills are introduced in Congress to permit the construction of a new bridge. The first bill, *Senate Bill 3499*, made consent for the bridge's construction conditional. The plans and specifications had to be approved by the Secretary of War and the Chief of Engineers of the War Department. Moreover, the plans must be satisfactory from the standpoint of the expected volume and weight of the traffic which will use the bridge. In contrast, *House Bill 10169*, introduced by Congressman Thomas A. Jenkins of Ohio, simply petitioned to build "in accordance with the provisions" of the Bridge Act of 1906. This plan stipulates that a bridge can be constructed as long as it does not obstruct the free navigation over the water or charge exorbitant bridge tolls. Furthermore, the Bridge Law stated that the Secretary of War possesses the power to force bridge owners to pay for any repairs or upgrades to the bridge. The Acting Secretary of War informed the House Commerce Committee that the War Department had no objection to the House Bill. As for the Senate bill, it was a different story.

If the War Department is required to approve such bridges from the standpoint of weight and volume of projected bridge traffic, some believed this would burden the department with additional duties and responsibilities. A modified bill is introduced by Connecticut Senator Hiram Bingham on April 26. Eventually, Congress agrees to consent to the legislation according to the Bridge Act of 1906. It is believed that the bridge company receives authorization to construct the bridge on May 13, 1926. Sadly, there was a snag.

When the bill reaches committee in late spring, it seems the wording in the bill has been changed to conform to "conventional phraseology" that requires listing the names of the states at each end of the bridge. According to an article appearing in *The Cincinnati Commercial Tribune* on

24

December 7, 1926, the clerk, in rewriting the bill, wrote that the bridge would be built

> "...between a point at or near Gallipolis, in the county of Gallia, in the state of Ohio, and a point opposite in the state of Kentucky."

Further,

> "...the state of Ohio or the state of Kentucky, or any political subdivision or subdivisions thereof within or adjoining which bridge is located, may at any time jointly or severally acquire and take over all right, title and interest in such bridge and its approaches."

The error is noticed only after the bill is passed and signed by President Calvin Coolidge. Subsequently, the bill has to be reintroduced and amended, causing a delay. The 69th session of Congress eventually passes the amended bill, much to the delight of the Gallia County Ohio River Bridge Company, just before Christmas. It is believed that the bridge company may have received the ok to begin construction of the bridge sooner if not for a geographical error by the congressional clerk.

In December, the bridge company is given a governmental form to complete. The document does not *require* the bridge's specifications, but it does *request* some particulars of the project, including a map showing the bridge's location, etc. The bridge's initial design is submitted on December 29, 1926, to the authorities in Washington, DC. The bridge company includes a map indicating the proposed location, a general sketch of the bridge in relation to Point Pleasant and Gallipolis, and the waterway for 1-mile on either side of the proposed bridge. The river's width where the bridge will be constructed is approximately one-quarter mile broad.

In addition, the initial plans offer a general idea of the length and height of the span and the position of the piers.

Before long, the bridge company awards the design contract to the J. E. Greiner Company of Baltimore, Maryland. Among the other designs of the Greiner Company are the

Market Street Bridge that spans the Tennessee River (1917), the Washington Street Bridge in New Castle County, Delaware (1922), the United States Naval Academy Bridge in Annapolis, Maryland (1924), and the Bellaire Bridge located upstream on the Ohio (1926).

But if community leaders and the residents of Point Pleasant and Gallipolis believe the ups and downs of the previous months are now behind them, they are greatly mistaken. The ensuing months will provide them with an equal amount of joys and sorrows.

As the new year begins (1927), yearly flooding from the Ohio hits the area extremely hard on both sides of the river. On January 11, one particular gauge places the river level at just over twenty-five and one-half feet. Two weeks later, local authorities are predicting that many of the streets in Point Pleasant and Gallipolis will be underwater, and they were. On January 26, the same gauge registers the river's depth at 50 feet. By the last day of the month, the river's level has fallen nearly 25 feet. Unfortunately, the reprieve from flooding is short-lived. On February 9, the water level of the Ohio at Point Pleasant is quickly approaching 28 feet. By month's end, the river has risen another 6 feet. On the 10th day of March, the gauge indicates a water level of around 17 feet. By the end of the month, the river's level has doubled.

Possibly as early as late winter, the bridge company receives word that its initial plans for constructing the bridge are rejected. However, the company is told their designs will be approved and a permit issued if the pier closest to the Ohio side of the bridge is moved 40 feet closer to the Ohio shore. The application is amended, the general plans are approved, and the bridge construction contract is offered for bid.

Sometime later that winter, possibly mid-February, community meetings begin being held. Most likely, the focus of the gatherings is to keep people on both sides of the river informed about bridge happenings and allow the community to ask questions of bridge leaders. Charles Evan Fowler leads the effort on the east side of the river. At about the same time, it is announced that the Pittsburgh firm of McLaughlin, MacAfee & Company, and the investment firm of Mackubin, Goodrich & Company of Baltimore have agreed to finance the bridge in the amount of $900,000. Moreover, the bridge company will be reorganized with many capitalists from Pittsburgh on the new board. There are informal talks being kicked around regarding a twin cities Chamber of Commerce.

As spring arrives, Greiner Company presents a bridge design using specifications set forth by the American Society of Civil Engineers. Designed using steel cables with stiffening trusses, the structure includes seven sections. The middle span is over 700 feet, and two spans on opposite sides of the main span, each measuring approximately 380 feet. Additionally, the design consists of an approach and an entrance ramp, each measuring over 75 feet, at each end of the bridge. While the bridge's total length is over 1,700 feet, less than two-thirds, around 1,100 feet, is actually over water.

The main roadway will sit on six piers. Resting on concrete caissons built on bedrock, three of the piers are water piers, two of which will be on the West Virginia side of the river. The remaining piers will be land piers, two on the bridge's western side and one on the eastern side. Constructed on top of the two central piers supporting opposite ends of the 700-foot middle span will be two towers, each over 130 feet tall. As initially proposed, twisted steel cable wires, similar to the ones used on the Brooklyn Bridge, will run the length of the bridge. A 22-foot wide, wooden roadway and a nearly 6-foot pedestrian walkway are proposed for the bridge's south side. The height of the road above the river's waters would be more than 100 feet at the low water mark. Finally, the designers also include a weight calculation, allowing around 1,500 pounds per car, the typical weight of a Ford Model T, and a truck gross weight of 20,000 pounds at intervals of 44 seconds in both lanes. It is estimated that the bridge could be built for $825,000.

As for entrances to the bridge, the east access to the bridge would lay at the 6th and Main Streets intersection in Point Pleasant. At the same time, the western edge will terminate on Route 7 in unincorporated Kanauga, four miles north of Gallipolis. This route is chosen because it connects with the new and improved highway west of Charleston. The proposed location of the bridge will not only make it a direct drive from Charleston to Columbus and points north and west but could significantly reduce the distance between the two state capitals by nearly 25 miles.

When the job is advertised, those companies wishing to bid on the job are given the option of proposing an alternative design. If the bridge could be erected for $800,000 or less, the company that wins the contract will receive half the money saved.

Before long, the General Contracting Company of Pittsburgh, Pennsylvania, is awarded the contract to construct the anchorages, bridge abutments, and piers. When the sealed bids are opened several days later, the American Bridge Company, a subsidiary of U.S. Steel, wins the contract and will oversee the construction of the superstructure. Among the American Bridge Company projects are several moveable bridges along the Panama Canal, over 75 bridges in the Philippines, and the 7th Street Bridge that spans the Allegheny River in Pittsburgh (1926). The Pittsburgh Drilling Company is awarded the contract to begin core drilling for the central water piers. The nearly 10,000 yards of concrete to build the approach ramps and the piers will be furnished by the Plymale-Wagner Company of Gallipolis. The Taylor-Meyer Company of Pittsburgh is chosen to install nearly quarter of a million feet of California redwood flooring on the bridge. At the same time, the Tri-State Paving Company of Wheeling, West Virginia, has been contracted to lay the composition of limestone and rock asphalt over the wood decking. Huntington resident, John Jenkins, has been chosen to design the toll booth, and the Skene-McAlpin Construction Company of Point Pleasant will build the booth. Another Huntington resident, Frank Martin,

Sr., will act as resident supervisor during the construction of the booth, which will be located at the entrance to the bridge on the Ohio side of the river.

As the winning bid for the contract, the American Bridge Company presents a new design to construct the bridge's superstructure that they believe will be both logical and economical.

First, the American Bridge Company recommends using eyebars instead of the traditional use of spun wire cables as the primary suspension system. Specifically, the bridge would be supported by a series of eyebars, flat steel bars nearly 2 inches thick, varying in length and weight, with drilled eyelets whose diameter measured over two feet at each end of the bar. Each eyebar is made of heat-treated rolled carbon with forged heads. The nearly 150 eyebars will be constructed offsite, brought to the site to be assembled, and then spaced according to the location of the eyebars on the superstructure. Placed end-to-end and joined in pairs of two with vertical hangers between them, a giant pin, nearly a foot long and weighing approximately 300 pounds, will then be run through the ends of the eyebars, tightened with a large bolt capped with a metal plate. The metal plates or retaining caps are about twelve and a half inches in diameter. The purpose of these end caps is to keep the elements (water) from the joint's interior. Specifically, the caps protect those areas where the pin goes through the heads of the eyebars and the hanger plates. Resembling a bicycle chain, the eyebars, with vertical hangers framed, will support the trusses and the bridge decking.

With nearly a century of use behind them, the eyebar design is not new to most bridge builders. In fact, the use of eyebars had been utilized a few years earlier by the American Bridge Company's parent company, U.S. Steel, during the construction of the Florianopolis Bridge in Brazil in 1924. While the Florianopolis Bridge is, by definition, a suspension bridge, it substituted eyebars as the suspension system instead of standard wire cables in the middle section of the structure only. In the case of the new bridge, the use of eyebars will be

29

used for the complete suspension system, end to end. Moreover, the Florianopolis Bridge uses double the eyebars, pairs of four per section rather than two as proposed for the new bridge over the Ohio River at Point Pleasant. This unique design translates into low redundancy and a greater chance that the whole structure would collapse if one eyebar gives way. Nevertheless, the American Bridge Company continues to propose using eyebars because they are less expensive in bridge construction but provide equal strength to the structure as wire cables. If utilized for the Point Pleasant-Gallipolis bridge, this will be the first eyebar design used in America.

To support the 700-foot middle span and to further reduce costs, the new design includes a novel way to anchor the eyebar suspension. The plan consists of driving no less than two hundred 15-foot steel piles into the ground around twelve feet deep near the approach at each end of the proposed bridge. Following, the eyebars will be connected to the piles, and the 200-foot long and over thirty-foot wide trough containing the piles will be covered with fill dirt to give weight to the anchorage. Lastly, the dirt will be covered with concrete as an added layer of longitudinal strength while also supporting the structure on both sides of the bridge. The anchorages will also double as a portion of the approach ramp to the bridge.

The plan proposed by the American Bridge Company also includes using rocker-type towers. Here, the towers will sit on a curved-shaped base, which would sit atop the two river piers. It was believed that this rocker-type design will allow some movement in the bridge's deck to compensate for the volume and weight of the vehicles. Additionally, the design will allow some minor movement in response to changes in the tension of the steel cables related to shifting loads on the bridge. In itself, this will give the impression that the bridge was swaying or tipping. As for the Greiner firm, it seems their original design plans have been overridden.

About the same time as the new plans are being proposed, a notice appears in several newspapers announcing the sale of $700,000 in bridge bonds. The 5,000 shares of preferred stock and 12,000 shares of common stock are 25-year bonds with a maturation date of 1952. With a minimum of 1,200 vehicles using the bridge daily, the estimates are that the bridge would bring nearly $135,000 in gross earnings during the first year of operation and around $163,000 by year five. A later notice indicates that the stock sale is going better than expected, saying that all the stock has been sold except for $50,000.

The good news seems to also bring about another change. The two groups working on different sides of the river decide to merge. The unified group will call itself the West Virginia-Ohio River Bridge Corporation/Company. While several of the stockholders in the company reside in either West Virginia or Ohio, the company also includes investors from Pennsylvania and Maryland. Because of his reputation as a proven leader, Dr. Holzer is chosen as the group's president. At the same time, Point Pleasant resident and president of the Marietta Manufacturing Company, Walter Windsor, who led the efforts on the West Virginia side to build the bridge, is welcomed as Secretary/Treasurer. Other members of the nine-member board include Carlyle Bartow, Henry Cherrington, Auville Eager, D. J. Gurley, W. M. MacAfee, D. J. McLaughlin, and E. J. Somerville. Board members MacAfee and McLaughlin represent the investment firm of McLaughlin, MacAfee & Company from Pittsburgh, Pennsylvania, while Eager is a banker and member of the Mackubin, Goodrich & Company investment firm located in Baltimore, Maryland.

In late spring, the American Bridge Company sends the proposed plans to Washington, DC, seeking a permit to begin constructing the piers. The plans are immediately rejected because they do not conform to the original plans already submitted. On May 2, the plans are resubmitted, and one week later, they are approved. And with that, the first of many contractors begin arriving in the Point Pleasant and Gallipolis area with their portable offices.

A few weeks later, a new division engineer is appointed who requests a set of plans and specifications for the bridge. Responding, the consulting engineers (Greiner) immediately sends the approved design, which called for a straight cable wire suspension system. Also included in the response is the alternative to constructing the superstructure: using eyebars. Upon receiving both plans, the original and the purposed, the new district engineer responds that no further plans are needed since Congress passed the bridge's construction authorization as part of *H.R. Bill 10169* in mid-May 1926. The bill is amended in late December and again in early March 1927. At about the same time, the Chief of Engineers and the Assistant Secretary of War sign-off on the bill. Under the direction of J. Wilson Richardson, resident engineer for the building of the substructure, the official construction of the bridge begins in May 1927.

During the last few days of May, the bridge construction may have had its first reported accident and nearly cost a worker his life. W. S. Childers, from Point Pleasant, is working from the top of a derrick when he loses his balance and falls. He hits his head on a piece of the machinery on his way down, knocking himself unconscious. The man then finds himself caught in some ropes underneath the water. A fellow worker, Charles Gilloman (sp.), from Australia, immediately dives into the water, gripping a knife between his teeth. The second worker is able to free his co-worker, and both men survive.

Despite the weather and the on-again-off-again work during the summer, the two water piers, the piers closest to the West Virginia and Ohio shorelines, are finished. In addition, General Contracting, who will oversee the construction of the bridge abutments, announces that things are progressing nicely. With the completion of the bridge's foundation just around the corner, it seems the bridge is closer to the installation of the steel. There is even some talk around the area that the construction is ahead of schedule. The bridge's opening could come as early as the following spring (1928). However, it may have been that the workers are simply trying to stay ahead of the upcoming winter weather.

By mid-September, the steelwork is on the cusp of being installed. The steelworkers have arrived, and the steamer

Ingersoll is on its way from Pittsburgh to Point Pleasant with tools and equipment. It is believed the company contracted to build the superstructure, the American Bridge Company, reminds the bridge's owners, the West Virginia-Ohio River Bridge Company, that steel eyebars will add strength to the structure and be less expensive. Needless to say, Holzer, Windsor, and the remainder of the West Virginia-Ohio Bridge Company Board are delighted.

The American Bridge Company is ready to commence the erection of the superstructure in November using the proposed method of constructing the superstructure (e.g., eyebars). But while the overall project is approved, the government reminds the bridge builders that the government reserves the right to require the American Bridge Company to make any changes regarding the bridge's safety or for the convenience of navigation on the river. This understood, the American Bridge Company, who had won the $400,000 contract to construct the steel superstructure, begin their work.

First, a temporary wire cable originating from a crane on one side of the river is pulled along the top length of the bridge's towers by another crane on the opposite side. When the cable reaches the opposite shore, a heavier line is secured to it, and the cable is pulled back across the river by the first crane. Thanks to the "pull method" between the cranes, the eyebars, varying in length from thirty-five to sixty-five feet and weighing between 2,500 and nearly 5,500 pounds, are then hoisted along the wire to their respective location in the top chain. Once in place, two vertical hangers are sandwiched between the two sets of eyebars. The pieces are then bolted together and connected to stiffening trusses.

The process continues with the eyebars from the anchorages being attached first and working toward the top of the middle span. The final eyebar connecting the span is not fabricated until the end of this phase of the construction process. As the top chain nears completion, the calculations for the length of the last piece are off a mere one-half inch! To remedy this, a small piece of slotted steel is made, put in place, and spot welded to complete the chain.

Once the top chain is complete, attention focuses on the vertical hangers, beginning on the structure's south side. Here, engineers place weighted drums filled with water on the ends of the eyebars to gauge the proper distance to the bottom trusses and chords and to equate the roadway's weight. When all the bolts to the horizontal and vertical chains are in place, the focus shifts to the bridge's north side and the same procedure. Following the installation of the roadway and the sidewalk, the bolts are given one last tightening.

During the bridge's substructure construction, the District Engineer allows deviation from the approved plans by permitting raising the top of the Ohio shore caisson nearly 10 feet. The District Engineer also allows dumping into the Ohio River of material resulting from the substructure's erection.

Considering the piers were completed in a few months, the talk now is of finishing the bridge and opening it for traffic by August of the following year…just in time for the 1928 auto touring season. By late December, it is said that the bridge construction is as much as two months ahead of schedule, despite the river reaching another record level of over 45 feet just before Christmas. Nevertheless, the progress on the bridge comes as good news, and Dr. Holzer begins sharing the word that the bridge may be ready for dedication on April 1.

As calendars are flipped to 1928, the bridge begins to take shape. In February, the decision is made to have the bridge coated with a silver, aluminum-based, protective paint. This would be a first in the U.S. The corrosion of the steel structure is likely as the acidity of the rain will be enhanced by local industries operating in the area. A resident of Gallipolis, John Leonard "Jack" Cheney, is hired to put the first coat of paint on the bridge. By most reports, Cheney rides his bicycle from Gallipolis to Kanauga to do the painting. Moreover, the last few days of the month see the second near casualty of the bridge's construction. On February 24, one of the workers on the bridge, Henry Small, falls nearly 60 feet from a girder on the span to the frozen ground below. Despite two broken jaws, a fractured skull, several operations, and "…after approaching the other world very near," Smalley survives and makes a full recovery (*Athens Messenger*, March 9, 1928).

As spring arrives, a preliminary date of May 10 is chosen as the day of dedication. The bridge's name is suggested to be called the Point Pleasant Bridge. Others want to name the bridge the Hoover Bridge in honor of Herbert Hoover, the current Commerce Secretary in the Coolidge administration. Still, others want the bridge to be called the "Silver Lace Bridge," a name derived from the silver paint covering the bridge and the lace-looking feature of the superstructure.

Around the same time Charles Lindbergh is making his solo flight across the Atlantic Ocean in the Spirit of St. Louis, the bridge is nearing completion. However, some minor work is not completed, so May 30th is chosen as the official dedication day. This date will allow the builders some breathing room to finish their work. However, there is growing excitement in the air. Before long, the one or two-day celebration has evolved into a week-long homecoming celebration planned for May 27 thru June 2. A third day, Memorial Day, adds to the week's celebratory mood. Subsequently, American flags began showing up on phone poles and front porches on both sides of the river. In addition, copies of the dedication day pamphlet are being distributed to all parts of the area with the caption "The Beautiful River's Most Beautiful Bridge" highlighted on the front of the program. The Point Pleasant Chamber of Commerce president and executive at the Marietta Manufacturing Company, Charles Oliver (C. O.) Weissenburger leads the effort. An article appears in the Sunday, April 22, issue of the *Charleston Daily Mail* inviting American Legion posts in Gallipolis, Huntington, Middleport, and Pomeroy to join with the Point Pleasant post in a special Memorial Day celebration. The event will precede "…the celebration of the formal opening of the new Ohio river (sp.) bridge."

On the west side of the river, the businesses are so excited about the planned activities they even have a motto. They call their celebration "A Riot of Colors." The city commissioners have arranged to have the streets washed and cleaned. Beyond a special sign that reads "Welcome to Gallipolis," the Elks and Masons will be holding an open house. Traffic plans are being formulated to handle the expected volume of vehicles, and extra officers are being hired to assist with traffic flow.

Most exciting, however, is the announcement that the bridge will be open for traffic beginning May 20 and last until the day before the dedication. As it should be, the honors of being the first to drive his car over the bridge are reserved for the resident engineer of the bridge's superstructure, Charles P. Vogel, of Huntington. It is said that Vogel took his drive on May 2, 1928. One can be certain that George Cumpston, the person in charge of the steelwork on the bridge, was nearby when Vogel made his epic run over the bridge. Wanting to get a jump on the next day's traffic, it is widely believed that the mayor of Point Pleasant, Milton Miller, is the first person to purchase a one-way ticket to drive across the bridge. The mayor makes his trip just before sunset on May 19, 1928. While Robert Heslop and James Robinson may have been the first to traverse the new bridge on horseback, it is widely believed that Mayor Miller's brother-in-law may have been one of the first to take a horse and buggy across the bridge. It is commonly believed that more than 4,000 cars drive over the bridge during the first twenty-four hours the bridge is open to traffic. In describing the appearance of the bridge's suspension, one newspaper writer commented that the eyebars resembled "…elongated dog-bones pinned together to make a chain."

———————

There seems to be something for everyone on the day of the bridge dedication. The day's list of planned activities begins with a 1:00pm parade through downtown Point Pleasant. The

Beni Kedem Shrine Band from Charleston leads the procession through the streets of Point Pleasant, across the bridge to Gallipolis, returning to the entrance to the bridge on the Ohio side where the parade ends. Also participating in the dedication parade that day is the St. Marys Citizen Band from nearby St. Marys, West Virginia, and a band from Chillicothe, Ohio. At 2:00pm, invited dignitaries take turns speaking from a platform near the Ohio toll booth, including Sen. M. M. Neely, the Lieutenant Governor of Ohio, and several congressmen and local officials. Dr. Holzer, president of the West Virginia-Ohio Bridge Company, is also among the speakers. Around 4:00pm, a $50 prize is presented to the best-decorated automobile in the parade from the West Virginia side of the river. Similarly, a $50 award is given to the best-decorated vehicle from Ohio.

Ohio Senator Frank Willis is noticeably absent from the list of dignitaries at the ceremony. He was instrumental in getting the bridge's legislation through Congress. Sadly, the first-term senator died on March 30, two months before the bridge is dedicated. A second person crucial to building the bridge, J. Wilson Richardson, tragically passes away five months (October 26) after the bridge is dedicated. Richardson, the resident engineer during the construction of the substructure, fell from the wooden scaffolding of one of the bridge piers being constructed for the bridge over the New River and drowned. He was 47. Walter Windsor, Secretary/Treasurer of the bridge company, will pass away a year later at the age of 41 (1929) following surgery.

Around 4:30pm, the daughter of Dr. Holzer, Christine, and the daughter of William Windsor, cut the celebratory ribbon. Afterward, a woman calling herself Miss Point Pleasant and a man from Ohio named Mr. Gallipolis meet on the span, and the bridge is officially opened. Everyone is then invited to make their way across the bridge toward Point Pleasant. It is also said that when the towboat W. C. Mitchell passes under the bridge during the dedication ceremony, the captain, Captain McDade, salutes by giving several toots on the boat's horn.

As an added attraction, a squadron of planes flies over the

bridge. This is followed by an airplane that drops two men who parachute to the ground. The day's activities end with a fireworks display and a dance in the Recreation Hall at the Ohio Hospital for Epileptics. Despite rain during the return trip across the bridge, the crowds are estimated to be around 20,000, the largest crowd ever gathered in Point Pleasant. One of those attending the dedication is a 10-year-old boy named John (Andy) Wilson. He is taken to the dedication by his father.

It is reported that Dr. Holzer no sooner makes it to the West Virginia side of the bridge on the return trip than he receives word that he is needed at the hospital in Huntington. There is also a report of a local accident as well. It is said that a Gallipolis volunteer assisting with traffic control is hit when a vehicle loses its brakes and hits the man, causing him to fall to the ground. The man receives only a few bumps and bruises. Local authorities report only 2 arrests at the bridge dedication, and both involve individuals being drunk in public. A vehicle carrying two couples from Xenia, Ohio, has an accident on their way to the dedication. No one is seriously injured, and the driver attributes the accident to rain on the road.

Before long, a plaque is mounted near the entrance to the bridge on the West Virginia and reads…

Gallipolis
Point Pleasant
Bridge
The West Virginia-
Ohio River Bridge Company
Pres: Charles E. Holzer, MD
Vice Pres: Walter A. Windsor
Directors
C. E. Holzer M.D.   Carlyle Bartow
W. A. Windsor   D. J. McLaughlin
Auville Eager   W. M. MacAfee
E. J. Somerville   D. J. Gurley
Henry W. Cherrington
General Contracting Corps.
General Contractors

The J. E. Greiner Company
Consulting Engineers
J. Wilson Richardson – Chas D. Vogel
Resident Engineers
A.D. 1927 – 1928

The total cost of the bridge is nearly $900,000, and approximately 97% of that is due to construction costs. Tolls across the bridge vary:

Foot passengers, one-way, 5 cents

Foot passengers, book of 20 tickets, $1.00

All passenger cars, 25 cents

Each additional passenger besides the driver, 5 cents

Additional passengers, book of 20 tickets, $1.00

Trucks, three-quarter-ton and under, 50 cents

Bicycle and one rider, 5 cents

Horse and rider, 10 cents

Horse-drawn moving van, including driver and one other passenger, 25 cents

Cattle, sheep, horses, hogs, etc., each 10 cents. Attendants at regular pedestrian rates

Only plain tread wheels allowed on the bridge

The excitement surrounding the bridge continues for some time after the dedication. It seems that newspapers continue to mention the bridge in nearly every issue published. In early July, Stanley Huntington, the owner of a battery shop in Gallipolis, is appointed to be the new superintendent of the bridge. The appointment comes during a meeting of the bridge board in Pittsburgh.

Merchants in Point Pleasant offer several prizes to the first couple to be married on the new bridge between July 5 and September 1. Prizes to the first willing couple to do so include a new hat for both the bride and groom, a set of dishes, four free Sunday dinners, and a tank of gasoline.

On July 20 at 3:00pm, a woman from Gallipolis and a man from nearby Rio Grande, Ohio, are reported to have agreed to the challenge. In addition to the bride, Bernice Balch, and the groom, George Stephenson, the only other people attending the ceremony that day on the far western side of the bridge are the bride's mother, the minister, Rev. E. C. Venz, and a newspaper photographer. However, the new couple will not receive the prizes provided by the Point Pleasant businesses. Unbeknownst to the couple, the land where the ceremony takes place is considered Ohio ground. According to the agreement forged between the two states, the West Virginia state line is the low watermark on the Ohio side of the river. Instead, the newlyweds will receive a gift offered by the bridge company. Two new couples, one from Ohio and one from West Virginia, take up the challenge several days later.

The first couple, Morris Wickline and Lola Johnson, are from Crown City, Ohio, approximately 30 miles south of Point Pleasant on the river's west bank. Rev. Porter from Gallipolis officiates. As for the second couple, the groom, Warren Sydenstricker, age 32, hails from South Side, West Virginia, located on Route 35 between Point Pleasant and Charleston. The bride, Mary Spears, age 18, is a resident of Mercers Bottom, a town located approximately 15 miles south of the new bridge on the river's east bank. The officiant at the second ceremony is Marcus (Mark) Shiflet. Known on both sides of the river as the "marrying parson," Shiflet has been known to contact West Virginia couples wanting to be married in Ohio, agrees to meet them at the entrance to the bridge on the east side of the river, and then travels with them across the bridge for the ceremony.

To accommodate two weddings on the same day, it is believed that the two couples arrive at a novel idea. The ceremony for the first couple, Wickline and Johnson, will take place on the back of a truck parked on the Ohio side of the bridge. When that ceremony concludes, the truck is driven and parked in the middle of the bridge span, where the second couple, Sydenstricker and Spears, climb onto the back of the truck. With the assistance of the minister from West Virginia, the bride and groom exchange vows. Sadly, history repeats itself as the low watermark of the river plays a role in awarding the prizes from the Point Pleasant merchants. Beyond the celebratory congratulations, the Sydenstrickers received the guaranteed prizes.

As expected, the novelty of the new bridge began to slowly wane. Still, the bridge's name continues to appear in countless newspaper articles. In one particular case, the story tells of a man from Gallipolis who jumps into the waters of the Ohio River, swims 20 miles south, and exits the river just before the Gallipolis Dam. Believed to be the first person to do so, the man completes the swim in less than seven hours. In addition, the article states that the swimmer is credited with being the first person to swim under the new bridge, passing under the span around 1:00pm the day of his swim.

Even as late as the fall of the year, news surrounding the bridge is still finding its way into the newspapers. In most cases, the issue centers on what the bridge should be called. Some insist the name of the Point Pleasant Bridge be kept. Others insist that the title the Hoover Bridge is appropriate. Still, others stand firm that the name Silver Lace Bridge is best. Most people, however, simply refer to it as the Silver Bridge due to its distinct aluminum-colored paint. In addition, the specially directed floodlights shining on the bright silver color at night allow the bridge to be seen for miles around. This helps to make a solid case for those in the last group. Whatever the case, all could agree that the bridge is "the gateway to the south."

––––––––––––––

About the same time the dedication festivities are being held in Point Pleasant and Gallipolis, a sister bridge connecting St. Marys, West Virginia, and Newport, Ohio, is nearing completion. Maybe not by coincidence, the St. Marys bridge hires the J. E. Greiner Company to provide the plans for the bridge and the American Bridge Company to construct the superstructure. Just as it had done in Brazil earlier, and most recently some miles down the Ohio River in Point Pleasant, the American Bridge Company chooses to employ eyebars as the critical element in the bridge's suspension system. In doing so, the Hi Carpenter Bridge becomes only the second in the U.S. to utilize chain-link suspension. On June 29, 1928, the United States District Engineer reports that the owners of the Silver Bridge have fully complied with the approved plans, and the work has been completed. Subsequently, the permit to operate the bridge connecting Point Pleasant and Kanauga is issued. Nearly four months later, the bridge at St. Marys is opened to traffic on October 28, 1928.

For the next thirty-nine years, the Silver Bridge, as it will be called, will remain in the news. At the height of the touring season in August 1932, a publication circulating in the area advertises the two cities located at opposite ends of the bridge. With the title "A Tale of Two Cities," the pamphlet includes a historical sketch of each city, a map of the principal roads, and pictures of several local landmarks, including the city of Gallipolis as seen from the Mound Hill Cemetery, a picture of the Silver Bridge, and aerial photographs of the Ohio Hospital for Epileptics and the Tu-Endie-Wei monument in Point Pleasant. Around 15,000 pamphlets are printed and distributed by the Community Club in Gallipolis and the Silver Bridge company.

The following month, a $6,000 damage suit is brought by a Point Pleasant resident against the West Virginia-Ohio River Bridge Company. The plaintiff alleges damage to her brick house during the piling phase of the West Virginia approach to the bridge.

It is announced that the West Virginia-Ohio River Bridge Company will have an exhibit at the 1933 Gallia County Fair showing the Silver Bridge and the surrounding area.

Meanwhile, the bridge company is sponsoring the first Mason County Day at the fair by arranging that all Mason County residents get in for half price. Not long before the fair opens, however, New York columnist, O. O. McIntyre, purchases a home on State Street in Gallipolis and presents the house as a gift to his wife, Maybelle, on the occasion of their 25th wedding anniversary. The house is two doors down from where Ms. McIntyre grew up and about a block away from the original home of Mr. McIntyre. For the first six months of the year, bridge officials report the heaviest traffic volume over the bridge since it first opened five years ago. It is believed that most of the traffic originates in North Carolina, South Carolina, and Virginia as travelers make their way to the World's Fair in Chicago.

—————————

Called by many the most significant flood to hit the area in history, the devastating January 1937 flooding of the Ohio River is causing many to wonder if the city of Point Pleasant should be moved to higher ground. Not only does the river level reach nearly 63 feet in Point Pleasant, but the record flood displaces nearly three-fourths of residents and damages countless businesses. Some reports are that waters reach almost two stories in some buildings during the fourteen days of flooding. The buildings damaged are the newly constructed courthouse and jail, a large hotel, the federal post office, two banks, and possibly five hundred homes. Ironically, the same year the Gallipolis Lock and Dam is completed some 14 miles downstream. It is reported that the dam's construction raises the normal pool stage at the Silver Bridge between 15 and 20 feet.

To mitigate future flooding, some local leaders suggest moving businesses to the northern part of the city, near the Marietta Manufacturing Boat Company, which is seen as higher ground. There is a large contingent opposed to this proposal, citing the number of historical buildings and landmarks, say nothing of the city's rich history of being located on the "point." A second consideration is building a flood wall for the downtown area since the federal government has offered over $1,500,000 toward such a project. Conversely, local leaders in Gallipolis seem adamantly opposed to building a flood wall in their city. Between 1949 and 1952, a nearly 30-foot floodwall is constructed on the eastern side of the river, hopefully shielding the city of Point Pleasant from future flooding.

Following the purchase of the Hi Carpenter Bridge by the state of West Virginia in 1937 and the removal of its toll charges nearly a decade later, the state seeks to purchase the Silver Bridge from the West Virginia-Ohio River Bridge Company for just over $1,000,000 in 1939. However, the complete transfer of the Silver Bridge from private to state ownership encounters a legal issue. It seems a lawsuit has been filed by several prominent Point Pleasant residents, and the final sale is contingent upon the lawsuit's outcome. Beyond the belief that the asking price for the bridge is excessive, the suit contends that the bridge will never become toll-free because of the cost of upkeep and regular maintenance, despite the sale of bonds to the public. Further, the plaintiffs contend that the city of Point Pleasant's tax base is not enough to fund regular maintenance on the bridge, along with the city's other expenses. In short time, the state supreme court favors the defendants and declines to interfere in the sale.

When the sale of the bridge is finalized and the transfer confirmed in 1941, the responsibility of inspections, care, and maintenance of the Silver Bridge, and many like it around the state done previously by the private owner, now shifts to the West Virginia State Road Commission. But before the contract is signed and the state takes over, the Greiner Company conducts a full inspection of the bridge in late December. Its recommendations include replacing the bridge's wooden roadway with concrete-filled, steel grid flooring. Before long, the job is awarded to the Perkins Bridge and Supply Company of Flushing, Michigan. It is being reported that the job will cost around $60,000 and should be completed before the calendar is flipped to 1942. The state of West Virginia performs a second, full inspection in 1951. The recommendations are to restore disintegrated concrete of the water piers, clean and paint the superstructure, and demolish the toll house. All the while, toll charges remain in place for the Silver Bridge until they are removed on the first day of January 1952.

Nearly thirty-five years after getting its original coat of paint, the bridge is given a second coat of paint in 1963. General touch-ups take place in 1964 and 1965. The pedestrian sidewalks are concreted and curbed the following year. Sometime in the next 12 months, the water piers are re-inspected with some slight deterioration in the concrete reported. Between 1960 and 1962, minor repairs are made to the roadway. Following established state inspection standards, the Silver Bridge is inspected in June 1959, January and December 1963, and January 1964. One of the 1963 inspections is performed by a welder and a black top inspector. Following the bridge's inspection in April 1965, nearly $30,000 of recommended repairs are completed. In 1966, runaway barges from upstream hit bridge piers. A subsequent report cites no damage. The state conducts two bridge inspections during the first eleven months of 1967 alone and a third on December 6. The maintenance engineer that performs the last inspection reports using binoculars to check the eyebar links and reports nothing of concern.

The Collapse

Friday, December 15
(Day 1)

In most respects, the weather around the Point Pleasant and Gallipolis area for the first two weeks of December 1967 is mixed. The first six days of the month see low temperatures in the 30s with highs from the mid-30s to the mid-50s. The skies are a mix of clouds and sun, and there has been no rain during the week. On the twenty-sixth anniversary of Pearl Harbor, the low temperature is an astounding 50 degrees while the high ballooned to a pleasant 60 degrees. As for the second week of the month, the daily temperatures run on the warm side for that time of the year. The lows each night hover above 40 degrees, while the daytime reaches highs in the upper 50s. Like the week before, there is no recorded precipitation. When Friday, December 15th arrives, the temperatures have become more seasonal. The high for the day is a chilly 37 degrees, and the nearly ten-degree drop in temperature from the day before only seems to add to the excitement of the Christmas holidays.

And because it is Friday, the traffic on both sides of the river may have seemed heavier than expected, thanks to shoppers searching for the perfect gift, people heading out for dinner, or individuals preparing to travel to Point Pleasant High School for the first boys' basketball game of the year. Moreover, the lower sales tax draws Ohioans to the east side of the river. In contrast, more liberal liquor laws and several good restaurants and shoppes attract West Virginians to the west side of the Ohio River. Additionally, it is believed that Point Pleasant residents commonly find more shoppes and restaurants in Gallipolis. It is thought that as much as one-third of all sales in Gallipolis are made by West Virginia residents. Conversely, the residents of Gallipolis enjoy coming to Point Pleasant because it has more of a small-town feel. This is to say nothing of those passing through either of the cities like out-of-state truck drivers and individuals heading home for the holidays.

In 1928, nearly seven hundred vehicles a day crossed the

Silver Bridge. The number of daily vehicles traveling was nearing 10,000 by 1967. Traffic has increased almost 40% on the bridge in less than a decade. Still, the original intent behind constructing the bridge is holding true, even after thirty-nine years: to provide the cities at each end of the span with an economic boom while acting as a source of great civic pride.

Charlene Wood is waiting to get on the bridge from the West Virginia side. She has just finished a short visit with her parents in Point Pleasant and is approaching one of the busiest intersections in town, Sixth and Main Streets. Finally, the light at the east entrance to the bridge turns green, which means she can continue her trip across the bridge to her home in Gallipolis. However, if Wood did not suddenly stop her 1964 Pontiac and shift into reverse, she could have possibly been on the bridge that tragic evening in December 1967.

Thomas Lee has made it past the light at the east entrance to the bridge and has progressed to the middle span as he drives west in his 1962 Chevrolet. A resident of Gallipolis, "Bus," as he was commonly called, played football at Parkersburg High School in his earlier days. In addition to being a window washer, he has been a shop employee of the G & J Auto Parts Store in Gallipolis for 25 years. In the summer months, Lee is the chauffeur for Mrs. O. O. McIntyre, the widow of the famed syndicated columnist. As one of nine children, Lee never married. He is the lone occupant in his car.

Directly ahead of Lee in the westbound lane of the bridge is *James Maxwell*, a 20-year-old upholsterer employed by the French Colony Furniture in Gallipolis. He is driving a 1962 Rambler with an Ohio license plate and is the lone occupant in the automobile.

Also in the center of the span, and driving a 1961 Ford owned by the Pickens Cab Company of Point Pleasant, is *Leo "Doc" Sanders*, a veteran who had served tours of duty in Korea and Vietnam. Just before 5:00pm on December 15, he radios to dispatch that he has just picked up a passenger at the Point Pleasant bus station and is taking the passenger to Gallipolis. A different driver is initially scheduled to take the passenger over the bridge; however, the driver is unavailable, so Sanders agrees to take him. As a married father, he and his wife, a Mason County school system teacher, have five children, all of whom live at home. Sanders commonly allows one of his children to ride with him, but this night, he is traveling alone in his cab, Number 13. In addition, Sanders is preparing to celebrate his birthday on December 20.

In Sander's cab is *Ronnie Moore*, a 23-year-old senior at Ohio University in Athens. He is an education major and has ridden the bus to Point Pleasant. His dad is waiting at the west end of the bridge to take his son home to Crown City, Ohio, a town about 40 miles south of the bridge, for the holidays.

Immediately ahead of Sanders and Moore in a 1965 Ford is *James Hawkins*. He is employed by the Firestone Tire and Rubber Company and lives in Westerville, Ohio, northwest of Columbus. Each year at Christmas time, the company hands out albums. As the youngest district manager in the company, Hawkins is returning across the bridge after dropping off Christmas albums at the store in Point Pleasant that was running low on them. Similar to several others on the bridge, Hawkins is traveling alone.

Next in the vehicles making their way westward toward the Ohio shore is driver *James Pullen* and his passengers, *Frederick Miller* and Paul Scott. All three men work for the New York Central Railroad and are on their way home. Pullen, the oldest of the three men, a veteran of World War II, and a 25-year employee with the railroad, is a conductor. Miller, 27, a brakeman with the railroad, is married and has two children, ages 2 and 4. Scott is a trainman. With Pullen behind the wheel, Miller is sitting in the front passenger seat, while Scott is seated in the back seat of the 2-door 1965 Dodge. Miller is a resident of Gallipolis, while Pullen and Scott live in Middleport, Ohio, some 15 miles north.

Weighing nearly 60,000 pounds and directly in front of the

Pullen car is a tractor-trailer registered to the Roadway Express Company of Winston-Salem, North Carolina, headed to Milwaukee. The vehicle is driven by Bill Needham of Asheboro, North Carolina. *Eugene Towe*, Needham's companion driver, is strapped in the sleeper compartment in the cab's rear. He is a resident ofCana, Virginia, a small town located north of the Virginia/North Carolina border. Towe has a wife and three young children and recently built a home and purchased a farm. He is planning for this trip to be his last as a long-haul trucker.

Having departed the freight terminal in Winston-Salem about the same time and headed in the same general direction, there is a second Roadway Express Company tractor-trailer directly ahead of the first one on the bridge. *Gene Mabe* is driving the nearly 52,000-pound tractor-trailer loaded with wiping cloths in large plastic bags, and the semi is headed for Detroit. As with the tractor-trailer behind them, a passenger in this Roadway truck, *Julius Bennett*, is strapped in the sleeper compartment. Both men hail from North Carolina. Mabe is from Jamestown, while Bennett resides in Walnut Cove, North Carolina. The two towns are less than 30 miles apart. Bennett celebrated his 31st birthday on December 7.

Also heading west on the Silver Bridge that day is the Howard Boggs family in a 1965 Chevrolet. The car is being driven by the wife, eighteen-year-old *Marjorie*. Along with Howard, a passenger riding in the front seat, is their 17-month-old daughter, *Kristy Ann*. The family lives approximately 20 miles northwest of Point Pleasant in Vinton, Ohio. They had not only been visiting family in West Virginia but had stopped in Point Pleasant to do some last-minute shopping for their daughter. Howard Boggs is a captain for the Ohio River (tugboat) Company.

The next car heading west on the bridge is a 1962 Ford Falcon station wagon driven by *Thomas Cantrell*. He works for Ohio Publishing Company and the Gallipolis Daily Tribune as a distributing agent. Today is his last day as an employee of the newspaper. Cantrell, a Navy veteran, is preparing to move to

California to be a cartoonist. He is crossing the river after delivering some papers.

Albert Adler is driving a 1965 Volkswagen heading west on the bridge immediately ahead of Cantrell. He is a graduate of Swarthmore College and is on his way home after working at the Goodyear Plant in Apple Grove, a few minutes south of Point Pleasant, as a supervisor of instrument maintenance. Adler is the father of two young children, ages 3 and 18 months. He and his family moved to Gallipolis from Philadelphia last year.

Immediately ahead of Adler is another tractor-trailer. Weighing nearly 65,000 pounds and hauling about 35,000 pounds of tire fabric in burlap bundles, each weighing between 600-700 pounds, the tractor-trailer is owned by Hennis Freight Lines out of Winston-Salem, North Carolina. It is driven by William Edmondson of King, North Carolina. He has taken over driving the semi in Beckley, West Virginia. Also in the truck headed to Detroit is *Harold Cundiff* from Winston-Salem. Cundiff was an Army reservist and served a duty tour in Korea. Unfortunately, he is asleep in the cab's rear.

Robert Head and *Ronald Sims* are next in the line of the cars on the bridge. The Ohio pier directly below them in the water indicates they are the last of the cars heading west on the middle span. Both men are returning home following their shift at the Goodyear Plant in Apple Grove.

Head holds a degree from the University of Chattanooga, is a 12-year Navy veteran and served during the Korean War, and is currently a production supervisor in the Fiber Foaming Division of the plant. Sims, a veteran of World War II, is a designer at the plant. It is believed that the two men are late coming home to Gallipolis this night because Head was waiting on Sims, who was working late. Although Head is the owner of the late model Pontiac, Sims is the driver. Head is the father of three young children, while Sims is the father of twin girls.

James White is alone in the car directly forward of Head and Sims. As the operator of a late model Chevrolet, he is

51

driving across the bridge to Gallipolis to pick up one of his sons, have dinner with him, and then bring the young man back to Point Pleasant High School for the team's opening game of the year against Ripley High School. Before coming to Point Pleasant as a teacher and coach, White's reputation preceded him.

White, an all-state athlete in football and basketball his senior year at Logan High School and an Army veteran, holds two degrees from nearby Marshall University in Huntington. Before arriving at Point Pleasant High School, he taught in the Logan County School District in southern West Virginia and Kyger Creek High School in Gallia County, Ohio. Along the way, White was a head football coach, an assistant football coach, head basketball coach, head wrestling coach, and head golf coach. During his four years as head football coach at Kyger Creek, his teams compiled a 31-4-1 record and 19-0-1 in conference play. In 1964, his football team went undefeated. White is popular with Point Pleasant High School students, who consider him a good dresser. Little did he know that his wife and two teenage sons were just a few cars behind him, but they are caught at the red light at the east entrance ramp to the bridge.

Charles Smith and his wife, *Oma Smith*, are west of the Ohio water pier. They are driving a 1965 Buick. Before his retirement in December 1966, Charles worked for the Chesapeake and Ohio Railroad for 27 years. The Smiths, parents of 7 children, reside in Bidwell, Ohio. They are crossing the bridge after visiting relatives on the West Virginia side of the river. The couple recently celebrated their ruby anniversary (40 years).

Immediately west of the Smiths on the bridge is a vehicle driven by *Marvin Wamsley*. With him are two passengers, *Donna Casey* and *Maxine Sturgeon*. Wamsley, the driver of the 1956 Chevrolet, is an employee of the Point Towing Company, while Casey is a part-time waitress at the Dance Restaurant in Gallipolis. Sturgeon is the mother of three sons, ages 12, 8, and 4, and three daughters, ages 14, 10, and 7. Casey is married to

52

a welder by trade, but he currently works in the office of a local taxi company. The couple has two children, a 2-year-old and a 10-month-old. Moments earlier, Wamsley passed his uncle, Frank, traveling in the opposite direction on the bridge. Marvin's uncle gave his nephew the friendly West Virginia wave.

On their way home from work and to the immediate west of Marvin Wamsley on the bridge is the driver of a 1961 Pontiac, *Donald (Horace) Cremeens,* and his passenger, *Alva Lane*. The two men have a great deal in common. Beyond working for the Marietta Manufacturing Company in Point Pleasant, both Cremeens and Lane served in World War II, Lane in the Naval reserves. Both the men live in Addison, Ohio, a few miles north of the bridge. Most striking, both Cremeens and Lane were born on January 22; however, Lane is five years older.

Stuck in traffic directly ahead of Cremeens and Lane is a Transcon Lines tractor-trailer. The truck has North Carolina tags and is driven by *Leo Blackman*, and with him is a co-worker, John Fishel. Blackman is single and resides in Richmond, Virginia, while Fishel hails from nearby Petersburg, Virginia. The total weight of their vehicle is around 70,000 pounds, and the contents of the trailer are most likely mattresses. They are headed to Indianapolis.

Gerald McManus of South Point, Ohio, is sitting west of the Ohio tower and driving a 1965, three-quarter-ton Ford pick-up. As the lone occupant in the vehicle, McManus, a foreman for a road construction company, is on his way home for the holidays after working at a job in Princeton, West Virginia. Once he reaches the Ohio side of the river, McManus has another 60-minute drive before arriving home.

Also sitting near the middle of the Ohio span is a 1959 Rambler station wagon with three occupants. In addition to the driver, *Margaret Cantrell*, there is her husband, *Melvin Cantrell*, and Melvin's friend, *Cecil Counts*. Melvin, no relation to Thomas Cantrell, who sits ten cars behind, is employed by the West Virginia State Road Commission. It is said that Mrs. Cantrell works at the Dairyland in Point Pleasant. Counts was done chopping wood on the West Virginia side of the bridge and asks the Cantrells for a ride home since they live close to each other. The Cantrells are parents to seven children.

Sitting just a few vehicles from the west entrance ramp, a tractor-trailer with North Carolina tags waits to exit. Registered to McLean Trucking, the individuals inside include two North Carolina residents, Francis "Frank" Nunn from Greenville, and Samuel Ellis, of Winston-Salem. It is believed they are hauling cigarettes. The two men are not the everyday drivers but are part of a last-minute crew called in to make the run.

Ahead of the McLean truck is a car driven by Paul (Mason) Hayman. In the 1955 Pontiac bearing Ohio tags with him is his new wife, Barbara. They have been married less than a year. Forward of the Hayman's is a 1960 Chevrolet bearing Kentucky plates. It is operated by Dewey McCleese. A native of Lewis County, Kentucky, and a U.S. Army veteran of WW II, McCleese is in the construction business.

The next car in line preparing to exit the 75-foot ramp near where the Ohio toll booth once stood is driven by John Fowler. Among his passengers in the 1967 Chevrolet is Betty Fowler, Buddy Fowler, Harold Craig, and Walter and Mary Nichols. Many in the vehicle are employed by Mason Furniture. The Fowler vehicle sits on the 380-foot Ohio span.

Conversely, the following six vehicles are located entirely on the west entrance ramp to the bridge. This includes a 1966 Chrysler driven by Ralph Belville. Ahead of him is a 1964 Ford. It is driven by William Ben (W. B.) Spann. Each is the lone occupant in their vehicle.

Three individuals are in the car directly ahead of Spann. The driver of the late model Buick with Ohio plates is Alfred Bingham, and his passengers include Kenneth Remita and Judy Chapman. All three are residents of Gallipolis, are employed at the Goodyear Plant in Apple Grove, and have been carpooling to work for several months. Chapman's father, Joseph, is the pastor at the First Baptist Church in Gallipolis, while Judy's younger sister, Shirley, is volunteering this evening as a Candy

Striper at Holzer Hospital. On this day, the fourth member of the Goodyear (Bingham) carpool, W. B. Spann has chosen to drive himself to and from work.

The next two cars within sight of the stop light at the west entrance to the bridge are a 1962 Dodge Dart, driven by Howard Rader, and a 1959 Chevrolet owned and operated by Clarence (Donovan) Sanders. Rader is believed to be an employee of the Appalachian Power Company. Similar to the cars driven by Spann, Belville, and McCleese, Rader and Sanders are the sole occupants in their cars.

At the head of the line of the 29 cars traveling in the westbound lane is Garry Meadows, a driver for Davis Wholesale Trucking, and his co-worker, William Murphy. The traffic light has turned red, so Meadows and his partner stop before exiting the bridge.

It seems that James Kidd has made it through the malfunctioning stoplight at the west end of the bridge and has turned south on Route 35. He is on his way home to Millfield, Ohio, after dropping off a load of Christmas trees in Huntington.

Meanwhile, heading east on the bridge, and the last car coming from the west, is a 1962 Ford station wagon driven by *Victor Turner*, an employee of the city of Point Pleasant. His common-law wife, *Maxine Turner*, and his 13-year-old niece, *Darlene Mayes*, are also in the vehicle. At 13, Darlene, or "Deannie," as she is called by her family, is a student at Gallia Academy Junior High School and is an excellent swimmer. Unfortunately, the same cannot be said of her uncle's wife, Maxine. She is afraid when the water gets above her knees. The Turners have picked up Darlene from her home in Kanauga and are traveling to Point Pleasant to decorate the Smith's Christmas tree.

Directly ahead of them is a 1965 Ford Mustang driven by *Hilda Byus*. Also in the car are her daughters, *Kathy*, age 10, a 5th grader at Ordnance Elementary School in Point Pleasant, and *Kimberly*, age 2 months. It is said that Hilda always picked up Kathy and would bring her home for lunch. After getting a to-go order at the Bob Evans Restaurant in Gallipolis, the three are returning home to Point Pleasant.

A 1965 International truck weighing 48,000 pounds and filled with gravel is ahead of the Byus family as they traveled east on the bridge. Driving the truck, owned by the James Merry Stone Company, is *Forrest Higley*, a veteran of the Marine Corps. who had been discharged in March after serving 13 months in Vietnam. In August, he married and is the stepfather of a 2-year-old boy. The family lives in Bidwell, Ohio.

Driving a 1959 Pontiac with West Virginia tags and positioned ahead of the gravel truck is *Nora Nibert*. Her passenger is *Darius Northup*. Like Melvin Cantrell, who travels in the opposite direction on the bridge, Northup resides in Gallipolis Ferry and works for the West Virginia State Road Commission. Nibert, a widow, is from Gallipolis Ferry and has 7 brothers and one sister.

Preceding Nibert and Northup and also heading east on the bridge are *Paul Wedge* and his wife, *Lillian Wedge*, in a 1961 Oldsmobile. Paul is a union representative with the International Brotherhood of Boilermakers and past Mason County School Board president. Earlier in the day, he had contacted his wife, telling her not to fix dinner. His plan for the evening includes picking up his wife at their home in Cheshire, Ohio, dinner in Gallipolis, buying a Christmas tree, and then attending the boys' basketball game at Point Pleasant High School, where their son, Jimmy Joe, will be making his coaching debut as the head coach. Their grandson attends the same school as Kathy Byus, Ordnance Elementary.

The next car in the line of eight heading toward the West Virginia shore is a 1955 Chevrolet driven by *James Meadows*. His passengers include his 2-year-old stepson, *James Timothy Meadows*, and James' mother-in-law, *Alma Duff*. James, a veteran, is employed as a dispatcher by the Point Pleasant Police Department. At the same time, his wife, Carolin, works at the G. C. Murphy store in Point Pleasant. The couple was married in March. Mrs. Meadows has not only purchased but wrapped all of the Christmas gifts planned for Timothy and placed them under the tree. All that's left on their purchase list is to get Timothy a cowboy hat and a toy garbage truck. Before going grocery shopping in Gallipolis, his parents dress Timothy in a coat with fur around the hood.

Directly behind the first vehicle in the line of vehicles heading east is a 1965 Ford. Two Point Pleasant High School teachers, *Denzil Taylor* and his wife, *Glenna Taylor*, are in the car. Denzil teaches business and typing at the school. His wife is on maternity leave, and the couple is expecting their first child in about three weeks. Moments before, the Taylors were at Holzer Hospital because Glenna was having early contractions. Beyond growing up as neighbors in Pennsboro, West Virginia, classmates in elementary, junior, and senior high, the Taylors attended Glenville State College together. They have been married for four years. Only days before, Glenna sent her parents a letter saying that this Christmas may be the best one ever. The crib for the new baby has already been placed underneath the Christmas tree.

First in the line of vehicles but still in the bridge's middle span is another dump truck hauling gravel. In fact, only four cars separate the two gravel trucks. The last of the two trucks is driven by *Alonzo "Lonnie" Darst* from Cheshire, Ohio. Traveling with him is Frank Wamsley, a weight man employed by the state of West Virginia. Wamsley has just passed his cousin, Barbara Hayman, and her husband, Paul, going in the opposite direction. In addition, Wamsley has passed his uncle, Marvin, also traveling west on the bridge. Wamsley waves to both the Haymans and his uncle as they pass. Darst, employed by the James W. Merry Stone Company, is in a truck weighing nearly 49,000 pounds. Darst had celebrated his 30th birthday six days before, and on December 20, he and his wife will celebrate their 8th wedding anniversary. Moreover, this may have been Darst's second trip across the Silver Bridge that day. Earlier, he had been taken to the west side of the river in a vehicle driven by his nephew, Steven Darst.

Just before sunset at 5:10pm, the light to the west exit of the bridge turns red. This causes the twenty-nine vehicles heading toward the Ohio side of the bridge to come to a standstill. Included in the line of vehicles are twenty-two cars, six tractor-trailers, and one pick-up truck. The last car in the line of traffic heading west is slightly east of the center of the bridge's middle span. As for the eight vehicles heading east on the bridge, including six cars and two dump trucks, the traffic is moving. The total weight of all vehicles on the bridge is nearly 487,000 pounds. And then it happens…

First, there seems to be a cracking sound coming from an eyebar on the north side of the suspension structure and immediately to the west of the Ohio tower. One of the eyebars seems to have cracked and come loose from the others. When this happens, the bridge's load is suddenly transferred to the adjoining eyebars. Momentarily, the pin holding the adjoining three eyebars and the vertical hangers comes free, releasing the eyebars from each other and causing the suspension chain to be severed. A collapse of the entire structure seems inevitable since all parts of the bridge's suspension are in equilibrium. Following a slight pause, the bridge span west of the Ohio tower collapses. Some of the span falls onto the Ohio shore, and the remainder falls into the river. As the structure begins to collapse, it is believed that birds nesting on and under the bridge quickly fly away.

Meanwhile, the eyebar suspension on the southside of the Ohio span collapses and falls upriver as the upstream suspension falls to the south. Within seconds, the two pieces fall on each other, trapping vehicles on the Ohio shore and on the Ohio section of the span. In an almost domino fashion, the collapsing deck then continues toward the West Virginia side of the structure. As for the middle section of the bridge, it collapses, falls upstream and to the north, and breaks into three sections. The east side of the center span falls directly into the water, sending 20 vehicles on the middle section of the span and all but 9 of the vehicles on the Ohio section of the span into the frigid, 43-degree temperature of the river below. As for the towers, the Ohio one falls to the north while the West Virginia tower is pulled into the river. In the meantime, a section of the east side of the middle span remains connected to the West Virginia pier. The east side of the West Virginia span falls straight down into the water on the east side of the Ohio. There are no pedestrians on the bridge at the time of the collapse. The bridge is gone in less than one minute, with only a few parts of the span above water. The remainder is submerged. At the time of the collapse, the river's level in the middle of the channel is around 35 feet, and the river's velocity is less than 2 miles per hour.

With daylight nearly gone, rescuers did all they could to help in the initial efforts to rescue people. At first, the only light comes from floodlights hastily mounted on trees near the water, car lights, and flashlights. Early efforts at rescue are first centered on land on the Ohio side of the bridge because the vehicles smashed by the bridge's superstructure are more accessible. Meanwhile, two workers from a City Ice and Fuel boat, Earl Hysell and William J. McCormick, manage to pull Paul Scott from the icy waters on the West Virginia side of the river. After falling into the chilly waters, it is believed Scott is able to stay afloat by grabbing onto a piece of lumber drifting nearby. As the workers in the rescue boat continue their frantic pace to rescue others, they find William Needham and William Edmondson and load them onboard the small boat. Needham has found his way out of the semi's cab by forcing his fingers into a small crack in a side window and pulling it down. As Edmondson is plucked from the icy waters, he lets go of a roll of rubber fabric, most likely, from his truck. The last of the four men picked up that night by the City Ice and Fuel boat is tugboat captain Howard Boggs. He is recovered more toward the middle of the river. Scott and Boggs have escaped from their cars, while Needham and Edmondson freed themselves from their tractor-trailers. As he is being pulled into the boat, Scott tells rescuers he felt he had to do all he could to get out of the river, so he could walk his daughter down the aisle in two weeks. The driver of the Hennis tractor-trailer, Edmondson, is in the river's icy waters for around 10-minutes before being rescued. Although both the cab of the Hennis tractor-trailer and the trailer initially stay on the Ohio bank, Edmondson asks about his co-driver, Harold Cundiff, who was asleep in the cab's rear.

A second boat from the Point Pleasant City Ice and Fuel dock saves a fifth person in the water, Frank Wamsley. His rescuers appear to have been Larry McDaniels and Wesley Wears. Harley Hartley is also credited with helping rescue survivors immediately following the bridge's collapse. Amid their efforts, those initially involved with rescue on the water also have to dodge trailers that have broken loose from their trucks and are floating downstream. Among those racing to the collapse site is Bill McCraw, the resident engineer for the Corps. of Engineers for the Huntington District, who is stationed at the Racine Locks but lives in Point Pleasant. He is at the Point Pleasant docks when the City Ice and Fuel boats begin returning with the survivors.

The five men rescued are taken to Pleasant Valley Hospital in Point Pleasant. Howard Boggs is admitted with cuts and bruises, William Needham with a fractured back, and William Edmondson has a broken arm and some scratches. The injuries to Paul Scott are not seen as critical. Also admitted to the Point Pleasant Hospital is William (Frank) Wamsley, whose vehicle is eastbound on the bridge and nearest to the West Virginia side of the river. Initial reports are that he has a broken back, but his injuries are listed as not critical. Edmondson, Needham, and Wamsley are all placed in the same room at the Point Pleasant hospital.

Also rescued following the bridge's collapse are McLean employees Frank Nunn and Samuel Ellis and Transcon passenger John Fishel. It is believed that the McLean semi fell nearly 75 feet. By the time the three men arrive at Holzer Hospital, the plea for all Holzer personnel to immediately report to the hospital has been issued, and employees have lined the hallways ready to respond. Frank Nunn is admitted with a back fracture and Samuel Ellis with multiple head and face cuts. John Fishel is admitted with second-degree foot burns. A fourth survivor, Margaret Cantrell, is also admitted to Holzer Hospital in Gallipolis. All four are on the Ohio span at the time of the collapse. Randall Moore is in the Emergency Room of Holzer Hospital at the time of the collapse with his uncle. Unbeknownst to Moore, his brother, Ronnie, is one of those on the bridge when it collapses.

In her diary, Shirley Chapman, a seventeen-year-old Candy Striper volunteering at Holzer Hospital the night of the collapse, writes…

> "This started out to be a great day, but it ended in tragedy. School went ok. I came home and got ready to go to the hospital. All went ok til 5:00pm. Then I heard someone say that the entire Silver Bridge had fallen in the river. I couldn't believe it, so I ran downstairs and there were sirens all over the place. Dr. Holzer asked me to stay and help. Thought of Judy coming home from work so tried to call home but the phones were dead. Finally got through on a pay phone and she had just gotten in hysterical. She had missed going in the water by 2 cars. She jumped out and saw cars fall in the river & pile on top of each other. I helped with ambulances and in one I saw 2 corpses. One was uncovered and a mess. 6 were brought in, 4 dead. Estimated 100 still in river…
>
> We went to see remains – awful. Start dragging tomorrow. Meth. Church set up as morgue."

All known survivors are rescued within the first 30-minutes

of the bridge's collapse. Any further efforts are hampered by the falling temperatures and ensuing darkness. Dawning their underwater gear, however, are two divers from the Racine Dam upstream who immediately begin an underwater search with little success. They report that many of the submerged parts of the bridge are shifting. Besides the frigid waters, the sediment on the river's bottom has been stirred up, reducing visibility to near zero. In addition, the river's current makes any work around the fallen structure dangerous.

Beyond the nine survivors taken to nearby hospitals, there are no additional physical injuries reported from the remaining eighteen individuals in vehicles located on the western end of the bridge at the time of the collapse. Despite the car dropping some 20 to 30 feet when the bridge fell, even those in the Fowler automobile are not injured. The list of eighteen survivors includes Garry Meadows and his passenger, William Murphy. Also included in the list are Clarence (Donovan) Sanders, Howard Rader, W. B. Spann, Alfred Bingham, Kenneth Remita, Judy Chapman, Ralph Belville, John Fowler, and his five passengers, Betty Fowler, Buddy Fowler, Harold Craig, and Walter and Nancy Nichols. The remaining survivors are Dewey McCleese and Paul and Mary Hayman.

Initially believed to be crushed in the collapse are three cars, the McLean Trucking tractor-trailer and the McManus pickup. Rescuers on the Ohio side of the bridge retrieve the bodies of five individuals whose vehicles have been crushed by falling steel. They are taken to the temporary morgue at Grace Methodist Church in Gallipolis.

The only surviving part of the collapsed bridge not in the water on the west side of the river is the approach. Its length is about 250 – 300 feet.

———————

Although phone lines on both sides of the river are busy that night as people check in with loved ones and friends who regularly travel over the bridge, word of the collapse reaches both Ohio and West Virginia governors, James A. Rhodes and Hulett Smith, within the hour. The West Virginia governor is notified by Paul Crabtree, a member of Smith's staff and a resident of Point Pleasant. Smith is attending a meeting of a 14-county citizens group seeking reforms in the State Road Commission. From the minute of the collapse, the absence of boundary lines that may have delineated West Virginia from Ohio, Buckeye State from the Mountain State, and east from west quickly disappear. The two have suddenly become one.

After completing her shift in the Pediatrics Unit at the hospital around 6:00pm, Gallia Academy High School senior, Shirley Chapman, decides to stop at the temporary morgue, Grace United Methodist Church, located across the street from the hospital. Entering the unlocked doors to the dimly lit church hall, she notices several covered bodies on the floor. On closer look, she reports seeing one body to itself. It has been placed within arm's length of a decorated Christmas tree.

Around 7:00pm, the Huntington District of the Corps of Engineers opens an emergency operations center. At the same time, McCraw contacts Dravo, the contractor at the Racine Locks, to prepare to send two 50-ton derrick boats. Around 7:30pm, Ohio Gov. Jim Rhodes appoints Gallia County Prosecutor John Epling to head operations on the Ohio side of the river. In short time, Epling crosses the river to the West Virginia side to organize a cooperative recovery operation between the two cities.

As Gallia County Sheriff Denver Walker assists with rescue operations on the Ohio side, Red Cross workers from Charleston and Cincinnati set up headquarters at the Skyline Bowling Lanes in Gallipolis. The volunteers begin serving sandwiches and coffee donated and prepared by volunteers from the Middleport, Pomeroy, and Kanauga areas. Cots are also set up to house Civil Defense and emergency workers. On the opposite side of the river, a few minutes later, the Mason County Chapter of the American Red Cross, with assistance from the Parkersburg chapter, begins providing food for the rescue and recovery efforts and assisting the state police in

63

operations at the National Guard Armory. Much of the food is donated by restaurants or individuals in the two communities. Food preparations occur at the Trinity Methodist Church in Point Pleasant and are delivered to the sites. Some food is being taken to barge workers by youth in the area. Volunteers also include a local pack from the boy scouts and ladies from St. Peter Lutheran Church in Point Pleasant. The latter volunteer at the canteens and the National Guard Armory. It is also being reported that at some point in the search, recovery, and salvage process Hennis Freight Lines sends nearly 600 cartons of cigarettes to be distributed among the workers.

The members of the Coast Guard unit stationed in Henderson, West Virginia, may have been some of the first groups to arrive at the collapse. Among the group is Jim Naegel, a member of the Henderson unit. He and other Guard members stationed in Henderson will spend the better part of the next two months participating in the search and recovery efforts. Before long, ambulances from both sides of the river and as far away as Charleston and Huntington begin arriving, as did local and regional newspaper reporters. A photographer from the Huntington Herald-Dispatch may have been one of the first photographers on the scene. It is believed that as many as twenty sheriff's deputies show up from Wayne County, in southwest West Virginia, near the West Virginia and Kentucky border. As often as possible around the site, firefighters from Point Pleasant are shuttled in boats to the Ohio side of the river. Members of the district Army Corps. of Engineers from Huntington arrive around mid-evening. By 10:00pm or so, the site has been visited by governors Rhodes and Smith, who quickly declare the area a disaster site after expressing their shock at the extent of the catastrophe.

Following the immediate rescue of any survivors from the night before, the attention then focuses on a three-step process. First, there is the recovery of the victims' bodies, followed by the removal of bodies and steel from the water. The latter act is delicate because there were times when steel had to be cut and removed to get to submerged bodies discovered in the vehicles. Finally, the third step involves searching for any remaining victims of the collapse.

Under the command of Adam Zabinski, commander of the Point Pleasant detachment of the U.S. Coast Guard, the Coast Guard assumes responsibility for all surface activities, controlling river traffic, and searching for victims downstream. The Corps of Engineers, led by William Falck of the Huntington unit, will focus on all matters about the bridge, including all underwater activity. Luckily, the Corps of Engineers had contractors working upstream on another project, including workers John Wallace, Roger James, and Joe Tavon. Subsequently, barge-mounted cranes are sent to the site within a few hours. A crew of divers will journey down the river with them. Collecting eye-witness accounts will be the responsibility of the West Virginia State Police and the Ohio State Highway Patrol. In addition, a West Virginia state trooper will take a position on each derrick boat. Finally, a member of the West Virginia State Road Commission will be on each barge to identify and mark pieces of the bridge structure as they are brought to the surface and loaded for transport.

The Chesapeake and Ohio Phone Company will install additional phone lines in the West Virginia State Police office in Point Pleasant to assist them in their duties. The headquarters for all rescue, recovery, and salvage operations will be located in the new courthouse in Point Pleasant. Meanwhile, the Corps. of Engineers will purchase over a dozen new outboard motorboats to assist local, state, and federal efforts.

Westbound river traffic on the Kanawha River is stopped at the Winfield Locks. In a short time, all barge traffic for nearly a 50-mile stretch above and below the bridge site is immediately halted from the Racine Locks south and the Gallipolis Dam north until further notice. Water releases from reservoirs on the river tributaries are cut back, including the Muskingum Conversancy Dam near Marietta.

Within hours, the Corps. of Engineers closes locks at several dams along the Ohio River between the headwaters of the river in Pittsburgh and the site of the collapse, including the Emsworth Dam, the Dashields Dam, the Montgomery Dam, the New Cumberland Dam, the Pike Island Dam, the Hannibal Locks near New Martinsville, the Belleville Dam, and the Racine Dam located less than 1-hour north of the collapsed bridge site. The latter was placed in full operation only 1-day before the bridge collapsed. Additionally, plans are immediately set to slowly close the dam at Gallipolis to reduce water flow around the collapse. However, the effect of the closings is not felt downstream for several days. Despite the aggregate efforts, it is believed that the river's level drops only three inches at Point Pleasant and Gallipolis.

Authorities also schedule an immediate inspection of the Hi Carpenter Bridge upstream in St. Marys since it was constructed using the same eyebar design as the Silver Bridge. State officials on both sides of the Ohio are told to immediately inspect all bridges along the river, beginning with the Chester/Newell Bridge connecting Chester/Newell, West Virginia, and East Liverpool, Ohio.

Initial plans are introduced to begin train service between the two river communities, using the New York Central Railroad and the train bridge located around 300 yards north of the wreckage. Similarly, ferry service plans are also being discussed to handle the nearly 4,000 vehicles that use the bridge daily. Until these plans are fully developed, drivers are being detoured to either the Mason-Pomeroy Bridge to the north or the new bridge over the Ohio River in Huntington. The traffic on the Mason-Pomeroy Bridge is being handled by state police officers. They are only allowing a certain number of vehicles to cross the bridge at any one time. In addition, the vehicles are being spaced apart.

With quickly falling temperatures, it is said that workers may have taken tires from some of the wrecked cars that landed on the Ohio bank and burned them to provide light and warmth during the early hours of the recovery. Likewise, it is not uncommon to see floodlights or headlights from cars shining on the area so rescuers can continue their recovery efforts into the night. It is also believed that local townspeople from the Ohio side of the river bring food throughout most of the first evening. Out of respect, many scheduled events are either canceled or postponed. The employees of the Pleasant Valley Hospital had planned a Christmas dinner at the Moose Lodge in Point Pleasant for Saturday night but postponed the dinner and gave the food to workers. In like manner, the Non-Commissioned Officers Club of the 3664th Coast Guard Unit of Point Pleasant decides to postpone their New Year's Eve dance.

Upon hearing the news of the collapse, the parents of Glenna Mae Taylor, Mr. and Mrs. Wilbur Grose of Pennsboro, and the parents of Denzil Taylor, Mr. and Mrs. Frederick Taylor, also of Pennsboro, arrive in the area after an 80-mile trip. They have told authorities they will stay in the area until both bodies are found. General operations around the collapse site begin to shut down shortly after 10:30pm. Assistant Secretary of State for West Virginia, John Musgrave, and his wife hear the news of the collapse while shopping in Huntington. They immediately begin to make their way to their home in Point Pleasant, but are stopped outside of the city limits and forced to show proof of their residency.

Several boats from the Huntington Coast Guard continue to patrol through the night. Officials are confident the death toll will soar. Additionally, around 30 units consisting of 200 men from all over Ohio and West Virginia show up at the collapse site before midnight. Possibly included in the list is former Marine and scuba diver Bob Campbell, who has traveled nearly one hundred miles from his home in New Martinsville. Another may have been deep-sea diver Lee Statler, who drove nearly 400 miles from his home in Nashville, Tennessee. For 16 days, 24 hours a day, men from the different groups stay at the site, 4 men on duty at a time, and ready to help wherever and whenever needed.

Moreover, the director of the nearly fifty-member Mason

County Civil Defense team, John (Andy) Wilson, is convinced it will be days before authorities learn precisely how many people were on the bridge when it fell. It is believed that the river's swift current may have washed countless bodies downstream. Other local and state officials fear the death toll could reach 200, making the collapse one of the greatest bridge disasters in U. S. history. Still, others are quick to point out that many of the cars on the bridge at the time of the collapse may have more than one occupant. Unlike a plane crash where the list of passengers is known, there is no way of knowing who is on the bridge when it collapses.

Criticism begins almost immediately from townspeople on both sides of the river and local authorities, saying the bridge was weakening, swaying at times, and getting too old for the volume and weight of constant traffic. It is said that even the mayor of Point Pleasant at the time, D. B. Morgan, banned parades across the bridge because of its poor condition. However, most of the main finger-pointing is directed at the West Virginia State Road Commission for neglecting the bridge. Many believe the commission had the power to do something about the aging bridge but did nothing regarding repairs, inspections, or general upkeep.

In addition to the criticism of the state road commission, many in the community have their own theories of why the bridge fell. Some residents claim to have heard a sonic boom from an airplane just before the bridge collapsed. The claim proves false when later investigation shows surrounding buildings are not damaged, and no windows have been shattered. Further, investigators check with the nearby military installations and conclude there was no aircraft in the area capable of producing a sonic boom. Still, others believe the tragedy can be traced to an event in April 1966, when 20 empty barges broke loose from their moorings upstream in Wheeling, freely floating downstream nearly 120 miles, eventually striking the Silver Bridge's piers. This theory is quickly discarded since the towers are the only remaining structures after the collapse. The yearly flooding of the Ohio and the construction of the Gallipolis Dam nearly 14 miles downstream, which may have raised the river level as much as 20 feet above the normal pool, are also possible causes. Some blame the bridge's collapse on the flood walls built on the east side of the river between 1949 and 1952. The construction of the floodwalls seems to have also increased the river's depth. Many believed that the infamous Mothman has something to do with the collapse. Some witnesses say they knew something was going to happen because nearly all the birds nested in the bridge's structure flew away the night before. The most historically-based reason for the collapse is centered on the "Curse of Cornstalk."

Legend has it that around October 10, 1774, the battle of Point Pleasant takes place between approximately 1,100 Virginia settlers who sought to settle in the area and about the same number of Native Americans who are trying to stop the English advance. During the battle, which some historians have referred to as the first battle of the American Revolution, Chief Cornstalk, the local commander of the Shawnee tribe, makes a diplomatic visit to Fort Randolph (Point Pleasant) in an attempt to make peace with the settlers. Eventually, the two sides reach an agreement known as the Treaty of Camp Charlotte. Three years later, as Cornstalk and his son are near the fort, they are captured. The chief and his son are subsequently murdered by English forces. Local folklore says that just before his death, Chief Cornstalk, still upset with the advancing settlers, swears a curse of death and destruction upon the entire Point Pleasant area.

Low temperatures hovering around 20 degrees and ice on the Coast Guard boats greet rescuers as they begin their work. The high for the day is not expected to reach 40 degrees, and a full moon throughout the night makes the morning even colder. Similarly, newspapers from the area began running headlines about the tragic event that had occurred the evening before. The *Charleston Daily Mail* led with headlines like: "Bridge Fell Like Card Deck; Fantastic, Witnesses Relate," and "Twisted Wreckage Marks Bridge Tragedy." Its sister newspaper, the *Charleston Gazette*, runs comparable headlines: "Pt. Pleasant Span Collapses: 70 Vehicles Into River" and "Now I Know What It's Like to Drown." The Saturday, December 16 edition of the *Chillicothe Gazette* began: "Witnesses Recall Horror of Bridge Collapse: Icy Ohio Searched for Bodies," while the local paper, the *Point Pleasant Register*, leads with the headline: "Silver Bridge Tumbles, Toll 70 Dead, 41 Missing."

As expected, the story makes its way into the national spotlight, and reporters quickly descend on the area from around the nation. It is reported that around 200 newspaper and tv reporters from over a dozen states make the bridge story their headline. While many of the larger cities in the U.S., including Atlanta, Chicago, and New York, send staff to cover the tragedy, one reporter may have come from as far away as London, England. True to form, most of the reporters are accompanied by a photographer. Film crews from the three major tv networks, ABC, CBS, and NBC, also begin showing up to report the tragedy. There is even a reporter from *Time* magazine on the scene.

Initial stories of the collapse varied greatly. An officer from the Ohio Highway Patrol shares with a reporter from the *Medicine Hat News* (Alberta, Canada) that the river's current was "very, very swift…" the night before. A second person tells the same reporter that he saw a boat going under the bridge at the time of the collapse. An article in the *Lethbridge Herald*

(Alberta, Canada) reports that as many as 75 cars were on the bridge at the time of the collapse. In contrast, another newspaper reports less than twenty vehicles on the bridge. The Sunday morning edition of the *Athens Messenger* says that the bridge first snapped on the West Virginia side near the eastern shore of the Ohio *(pg. 1)*. "One of the deceased," says the *Kerrville* (Texas) *Daily Times*, "has been identified as George McManus of Southside, West Virginia" *(pg. 10A)*. "Divers searching the waters of the Ohio Saturday," records the *Independent Press-Telegram*, Long Beach, California, in its December 17 issue, "found 57 vehicles-40 cars and 17 trucks-which had plunged from the bridge" *(pg. 9)*. *The Herald-Tribune*, Sarasota, Florida, reports "...there were-at the minimum-57 persons trapped beneath the surface *(pg. 1)*. Some tv newscasters tell their viewers that as many as 60 to 75 vehicles were on the bridge when it collapsed. Meantime, the basement of the Mason County Courthouse becomes the press headquarters.

Things are disorganized at first, and confusion reigns around the recovery area. Individuals on both sides of the river ask anyone in a uniform for information regarding loved ones and overdue relatives. Reporters are getting in the way of workers trying to do their work, and the West Virginia State Police arrest 3 newscasters for hindering operations. One arrest came in the early afternoon when a tv crew from Washington, DC, appeared on one of the dredges. They were later released, and no charges were filed. With limited housing in the area, reporters who are lucky enough take up residence in local hotels, motels, or boarding houses. Those not so fortunate are forced to sleep in their cars. At the same time, excessive traffic makes it difficult for heavy equipment and emergency vehicles to arrive.

In her diary's December 16th entry, high school senior Shirley Chapman shares her poignant thoughts on the last 12 hours.

> *"I got up at 7:45 this morning – couldn't sleep. Went to church to help decorate and dust...Went to Silver*

Bridge. It looked worse in daylight. We went clear down to water (against cops wishes). They had started dragging."

The first of two news briefings are held in the early afternoon. A second briefing, led by Col. Falck, takes place around 3:00pm. Nearly 100% of all known information is released to the press. The press is told that the Corps.' contracted equipment list includes two 50-ton and two 20-ton derrick boats, five launches, and two self-propelled needle flat boats. The needle boats will be used to sound the water with fathometers. The derrick boats include cranes with clamshell buckets to remove vehicles and steel from the river. The towboat from the Dravo Corporation, the Constructor, will be used to position the derrick boats hauling the 50-ton cranes. The Corps. expects the towboat, Robert G. West, to arrive shortly to assist in positioning the cranes. Two towboats from the M. T. Epling Company, the Panza and the Trojan, accompany two 20-ton derrick boats. Eventually, these cranes will move south of the collapse site to investigate any new findings uncovered by divers. After they have recovered all vehicles from the water, the Dravo derrickboats will be used to remove sections of steel from the site of the collapse. The smaller Epling cranes will not be used because of their limited lifting ability. A Corps. derrickboat will be used to unload the recovered steel. Additionally, the two bigger derrickboats and their crews will work 24 hours a day, while the Epling boats will work two, 12-hour shifts.

By 2:00pm, the towboats Panza and Trojan are in place, ready to begin operations on the east side of the Ohio. Around 4:00pm, the Dravo derrick boats, accompanied by the towboat Constructor, arrive from the Racine Locks and begin operations near the western side of the river. Just before the Corps. towboat Robert G. West arrives with another derrick and some barges from Marietta, three additional divers from the Pittsburgh district arrive. Two additional boats, one from Sutton and one from Summersville, West Virginia, are also being dispatched to the site of the collapse.

In return for professional courtesy, the press is asked to abide by respectful yet straightforward rules. First, reporters are told not to take photographs of any recovered bodies. Next, authorities plead with reporters not to get in the way of recovery workers performing their duties. Finally, it is shared that the five bodies recovered on the Ohio section of the span on Friday night remain at the Grace Methodist Church in Gallipolis, awaiting identification. The church is located across the street from the hospital.

By 12:00noon, Charles Scheffey, from the Bureau of Roads (Federal Highway Administration) division, has arrived from Washington to work closely with federal highway people. Around the same time, the first of dozens of divers on hand to assist with the recovery efforts are sent into the river to conduct a general viewing of the collapsed area. After nearly six hours, they return to the surface and report seeing bodies in the cars. One diver says the bridge seems to have landed upside down on the vehicles, forming almost a cage over many of them. As a result, it will be nearly impossible to retrieve bodies until the bridge's steel parts are removed. Some divers report seeing drivers still clutching the steering wheel with their hands. The task of marking vehicles and extracting bodies will begin the next day, Sunday, December 17.

Not long into the afternoon, the Red Cross contacts the Trinity Methodist Church on Viand Street in Point Pleasant, requesting the use of the church's kitchen as a center to prepare food for workers at the disaster site. It is said that the lights in the church's kitchen and social hall stayed on continuously until December 29.

Just before sunset, divers from Marine Contracting Incorporated, located in Southport, Connecticut, arrive by plane at the recently opened Mason County Airport. In addition to the twenty-one-man crew flown from Southport, a second crew is called in from New Orleans to assist with deep-water recovery and salvage operations. Upon arriving, divers are told that at least 50 are presumed dead. Just as many cars, trucks, and buses are believed to be in the water. Full-scale operations are expected to begin when all the divers from Marine Contracting and their equipment have arrived, and there are safe water conditions.

The plan is for divers to work in two 12-hour shifts, with as many as six to a team. This will include deep-sea divers. As the divers from Marine Contracting International locate vehicles, the derrick boats move into place. All divers will be allowed to stay in the water for about an hour before they are required to come to the surface. After a rest period, they will be allowed to resume their efforts. To stay warm in the 40-degree water, hot water will be pumped into the suits of deep-sea divers so they can better withstand the chilling waters of the Ohio River. The heating of the suits is controlled by compressors on barges located on the surface. Beyond wearing headlights on their masks in the murky waters, divers will wear weighted suits and padded gloves and rely on touch to find victims. Deep-sea divers will have a radio transmitter attached to the side of their helmets to communicate with those on the barge above. Even though there is a chance that it will damage a piece of steel that may give a clue to the cause of the collapse, underwater torches will be used to cut open car doors or metal to retrieve bodies. Buck Hale, a master diver, has been called to coordinate all diving operations.

By early evening, both workers and equipment have arrived so that the initial search and recovery efforts could begin the following day. This includes over 75 workers and supervisors, over a dozen divers, and countless pieces of equipment.

Early on, it becomes clear to everyone on both sides of the river that this was not the first time the Huntington District of the Corps. had been called into a recovery situation, and they are right! Sixty-three years to the day, December 15, 1904, the members were called to Charleston, West Virginia, because a suspension bridge had collapsed into the Elk River. The collapse kills 2 and injures six children on their way to school in a horse-drawn wagon. The collapse is traced to a fracture in

74

the bridge's suspension. As a result of the fracture, the bridge's roadway is tilted, and the passengers and the wagons fall into the icy river. Moreover, the strain snaps one of the cables on the lower side of the bridge, causing the roadway to flip onto those on the bridge.

When a body is located in a vehicle, plastic bleach or milk containers donated by local residents are used as buoys to mark the location. Following, divers hook a cable onto a secure part of the vehicle, such as an axle. The vehicle is then lifted from the water by a clamshell bucket on a crane. According to LTJG Joe Mason, one of the first members from the Huntington unit of the Coast Guard to arrive on the scene and who spent 61-days in the area of the collapse, the recovery process is solemn.

The vehicle is brought to a nearby barge. Bodies are then placed in a bag, transferred to Mason's boat, and then taken to the West Virginia side of the river. Upon reaching the eastern shore, Mason and his crew, Chief Petty Officer William E. Jones, Seaman Daniel Escobar, and Engineman First Class Lewis, respectfully give the body to West Virginia State Police members. The state police place the body in an awaiting ambulance and accompany the body to the temporary morgue at the National Guard Armory in Point Pleasant for identification. Several volunteer nurses at the morgue assist in receiving the body and are on hand to help the Mason County coroner, Dr. Oliver Eschenaur. All along the process, a member of the West Virginia State Police is on a boat nearby to record the type of vehicle recovered and the number of bodies inside.

By day's end, it is being reported that nearly 60 individuals, including LTJG Mason and his crew, have taken up residency in the Point Pleasant Resort, a property owned by the U.S. Small Business Corporation. The resort was opened in 1965, but the Small Business Corporation acquired the property in 1966 at a public sale after the original owners encountered money issues. Many of the rooms at the resort have neither heat nor running water.

Moreover, local clergy on both sides of the Ohio offer their pastoral services to the community. They are on hand at the Point Pleasant Armory for grief counseling and to assist individuals with their physical and emotional needs. Workers at the Gallipolis Dam, located nearly 15 miles downstream, report seeing debris from the wreckage in the waters.

For the next several weeks, porch lights are turned on as a sign of respect for those that lost loved ones and friends in the collapse. Moreover, the porch lights remain on to display the respect and love between the two communities.

With less than 10 hours of daylight each day, work at the site of the collapse begins in earnest not long after sunrise, despite the presence of several floodlights. The first order of business at the press briefing may have been an update on the death toll, which now stands at five. The names of the deceased include Leo Blackman, recovered from the cab of the Transcon tractor-trailer. The tractor-trailer seems to have been halfway between the Ohio tower and the Ohio approach when the bridge fell. Also declared deceased from the initial collapse are Melvin Cantrell and his passenger, Cecil Counts, Gerald McManus, and a female as yet unidentified. Immediately after recovering the five bodies, they are taken directly to a temporary funeral home on the Ohio side of the river.

With a headline reading "2nd Bridge Disaster of the Year," the *Herald-Advertiser* runs a syndicated article that includes a short history of bridge failures over the past twenty-five years. The article begins by citing the collapse of a bridge near Mexico City that happened eleven days before the Silver Bridge tragedy. Other bridge failures mentioned in the article include the 1956 train bridge tragedy in India, the collapse of a bridge in China that killed around 200 individuals, and the fracture of a train bridge in Brazil that killed about 100. Both of the latter collapses happened within 6 months of each other in 1950. Additionally, the article mentions the failure of a bridge that took the lives of around 150 individuals in Japan in 1948 and the 1947 tragic failing of the Pauna Bridge in Colombia that sent some 50 people to their death. The article closes with three paragraphs that mention the epic collapse of the Tacoma Narrows Bridge in Washington state on November 7, 1940. Before its destruction, the bridge laid claim to being the third longest bridge in the world. Locals called the bridge "Galloping Gertie" because high winds gave the bridge a swaying motion. At the time of the tragedy, the nearly 2,800-foot bridge spanning Puget Sound was less than six months old.

There were no deaths reported.

Authorities also report that the number of vehicles on the bridge at the time of the collapse has been reduced to around 50, and the number of persons missing adjusted to less than 60. Additionally, leaders at all levels of government believe the first collapse originated on the Ohio side of the bridge but add that the structure's failure is in no way connected to the anchorages. The anchorages remain securely in place. It is also reported that the arduous task of removing vehicles from the water will begin today. At some point during the early hours of the day, the Federal Highway Administration announces the NTSB will not only assume direction for the investigation but seek to determine a cause for the collapse. Admiral Louis Thayer will lead the investigation phase of the inquiry.

The issue of ferry and train commuter services is being explored as possible solutions to traffic issues. Once the ferry service is selected, it must be ok'd by the Coast Guard. In addition, ramps for landing the ferry must be chosen and construction undertaken. Permission has been granted by Point Pleasant authorities to use the end of Fourth Street or Main Street as two possible landing areas. Kanauga officials have ok'd four potential landing sites. To assist students who live in Point Pleasant and attend Kyger Creek High School in nearby Cheshire, Ohio, Walter Windsor, president of the Marietta Manufacturing Company, has offered to shuttle them across the river using a company-owned boat. Finally, no fewer than 30 towboats and barges are backed up on both sides of the collapsed bridge, and the list seems to be growing. With all known survivors rescued, the efforts now shift to recovery.

The area clergy report increased church attendance as worshippers gather to remember friends and loved ones lost in the tragedy. One minister decides to forego the scheduled opening hymn, "Hark, the Herald Angels Sing," and replace it with "O God, Our Help in Ages Past." The pews are packed with worshippers at the First Baptist Church in Gallipolis, where Rev. Joseph Chapman is the pastor. In her December 17th diary entry, Shirley Chapman writes that her sister,

Judy,…

"…spoke in the opening and almost cried. Church was really great. Many came forward at the invitation for salvation and prayer…"

By mid-day, the traffic, comprised chiefly of sightseers on the river's Ohio side, is reportedly backed up for nearly five miles on Ohio Route 7. Police cars equipped with loudspeakers are being used for crowd control. It is hoped that opening the I-77 bridge connecting Williamston, West Virginia, and Marietta, Ohio, will relieve the congestion. As yet unopened, the formal dedication of the bridge was to occur the next day, Monday, December 18.

With a workforce of around 65 men, the task of locating vehicles and bringing them to the surface begins early in the day. Divers on the "A" shift report that the river's current is swift and worsening. In response, large metal shields are lowered into the water to deflect the current around the divers. In addition, the river's 40-degree temperature is making the divers cold even with their protective equipment. Nevertheless, the divers move east from the Ohio shore toward the West Virginia side of the river.

Around 4:30am, the first vehicle is brought to the surface and is believed to be leaking gas. It is a 1961 Oldsmobile with West Virginia tags and two bodies inside. However, only one of the bodies makes it to the recovery barge. The recovered body is that of a middle-aged male. A few hours after sunrise, a second vehicle, a 1959 Pontiac also with West Virginia plates, is brought to the surface. The car contains the bodies of two middle-aged individuals, a male and a female. The clamshell-equipped crane brings a third vehicle to the surface less than an hour later. Bearing a West Virginia license, the 1962 Ford station wagon contains the bodies of a middle-aged man and a teenage girl. There are reports that there may have been a third person in the car at the time of the collapse, a middle-aged woman.

Throughout the day, loved ones and friends continue to

contact local authorities regarding individuals that may have been on the bridge when it fell. Dr. W. F. White, a dentist in Ravenswood, calls to check on his brother, James.

Around 6:00pm, the body of a young male is recovered in the cab of a Roadway truck. The deceased is discovered nearly one thousand yards downstream from the wreckage. An amphibian "duck" donated for use by the Belle (West Virginia) Fire Department transports the body to the West Virginia shore. The body is tagged and taken to the temporary morgue for proper identification. And just before 8:00pm, a fourth vehicle is brought to the surface. Two middle-aged males are inside the 1961 Pontiac. The car bears an Ohio license plate.

This brings the total of bodies recovered to 12 and recovered vehicles to nine. As many as thirty or forty persons are still listed as missing. Beyond the five recovered vehicles on the western approach to the bridge, three of the remaining vehicles recovered are found near the middle section of the collapsed bridge and west of the West Virginia tower. The fourth is retrieved on the Ohio side of the span.

Questions arise about who might be responsible for the tragedy: the state of West Virginia or the federal government since Route 35 is a federal highway. West Virginia authorities quickly point out that under present laws, $20,000 is the maximum that can be collected for each life lost.

Monday, December 18
(Day 4)

The chalk blackboard at the Mason County Courthouse in Point Pleasant is updated as the day begins. Besides the names of the five deceased individuals announced on Saturday, the updated list includes Donald Cremeens, Alva Lane, Darlene Mayes, Nora Nibert, Darius Northup, Robert Towe, Victor Turner, and Paul Wedge. Towe, a co-driver with William Needham in one of the Roadway tractor-trailers, would have celebrated his 34th birthday on January 21. The total recovered and identified bodies currently stands at 13, possibly as many as 40 or more unaccounted for or missing.

About the same time divers on the "A" shift find vehicle wreckage about 60 feet east of the Ohio abutment, workers on the opposite side of the river bring to the surface a 1955 Chevrolet. The car is discovered not far from the West Virginia pier and contains three bodies. Inside are a middle-aged woman, a young man possibly in his late 20s or early 30s, and a young child. The child is dressed in a winter coat with fur around the collar.

Possibly around midday, Mason County's Civil Defense director Wilson orders all roads into Point Pleasant blocked. The directive is given to reduce the volume of outside traffic coming into the city. Although nearly 1,000 vehicles are turned away, the move angers local merchants who complain of the negative effect on Christmas sales. This comes not long after Ohio Governor Rhodes and West Virginia Governor Smith agree to close the St. Marys bridge following a recommendation from Hardesty and Hanover, an engineering firm from New York.

Following their 3-day stay, Margaret Cantrell, Samuel Ellis, and John Fishel are discharged from Holzer Hospital. Meanwhile, William Needham is released from Pleasant Valley Hospital at about the same time. While Bill Edmondson will remain at Pleasant Valley Hospital until after Christmas, Frank Wamsley will stay longer. Following his release from

Holzer Hospital, Frank Nunn is forced to wear a back brace for several more weeks.

News reaches the community around 2:00pm that the female body recovered on Sunday has been identified as Lillian Wedge, wife of Paul Wedge. Her body is one of the first bodies to be recovered outside of a vehicle. Many local newspapers' afternoon editions began listing the obituaries or funeral plans for bridge victims. The funeral service for 40-year-old Melvin Cantrell will be held today in the chapel of the Crow-Hussell Funeral Home on Jefferson Boulevard in Point Pleasant, beginning at 2:00pm. Rev. Don McMillen will officiate, and burial to follow at Suncrest Cemetery.

Following the funeral, a freelance writer from northeast Ohio and a recent graduate of Ohio University in nearby Athens, Ohio, describes Cantrell's funeral in an article, saying that Mr. Cantrell was buried in a simple casket, was a former employee of the West Virginia State Road Commission, and was part of the crew that performed repairs on the Silver Bridge in 1965. Despite being sedated, the writer says that Mrs. Cantrell is temporarily released from Holzer Hospital just long enough to attend her husband's funeral. Mr. Cantrell's mother reportedly screams throughout most of the funeral service. The writer continues the article by recording that many who attended the funeral wore blue jeans and faded shirts, and many of the family members sang songs with stern and sad expressions. The writer concludes his story by adding that Mr. Cantrell was very poor, lived in a four-room shack with his wife and seven children, had no insurance, and his passing leaves the family penniless.

The bodies of three of the deceased are being returned to their chosen locations, including Gerald McManus to South Point, Ohio, and Cecil Counts to Grayson, Kentucky. The body of Leo Blackman will be transported to Richmond, Virginia, and the interment will take place at Green Hill Cemetery in Buena Vista, Virginia. On his death certificate, the coroner records the length of Blackman's stay at the place of death (Kanauga) as "minutes."

Near sunset, it is announced that permission has been granted to begin ferry service between Point Pleasant and Gallipolis. One company that applies for the license is Point Towing Company of Point Pleasant…the same company that employs Marvin Wamsley.

At the same time, a small plane with a dad and his three children on board makes a crash landing in a field near Shadyside, Ohio. The family had taken off from their home in Wharton, New Jersey, earlier in the day to fly over the collapsed bridge site. The father hopes to land the plane in Point Pleasant and refuel, but the airport does not have the proper fuel for the aircraft. As the plane is returning to New Jersey, the pilot, the father, radios the tower at the Wheeling Airport around 5:00pm that the aircraft has run out of gas. Despite his attempt to make it to the airport, the father is forced to make a belly landing in a vacant lot. Everyone on the aircraft, including the dad, and the three kids, ages 10, 9, and 7, walk away with only minor cuts and bruises.

As the recovery work continues into the evening, divers report that no vehicles have been found between the West Virginia tower and the shoreline. However, a 1965 Buick, recovered on the western side of the river and bearing Ohio plates, is brought to the surface around 9:00pm. The car contains the bodies of an older male and an older female. Both are found in the car some 400 feet downstream on the Ohio side of the river. As with the other bodies, the vehicle's location is noted and taken to shore. The bodies are removed from the car, tagged, and the bodies are transported to the National Guard Armory in Point Pleasant.

The Corps. of Engineers decides to begin 24-hour operations to step up recovery as local volunteers continue to drag the river for bodies. Similarly, some preliminary work has already started bringing parts of the bridge structure to the surface. As parts of the bridge are recovered, the location of the recovered part is noted by a representative of the West Virginia State Road Commission, numbered, and loaded onto waiting barges. All the while, divers in the water and workers on the surface are told to watch for any parts of the bridge that appear to be broken or severed.

During the late-night operations, local authorities are notified that an eyebar has been recovered between the Ohio tower and the western shoreline of the river, and it's found to have a fracture across one of the ends. In addition, a section of one of the round ends is missing. It is believed to be eyebar N330. Installed on the north side of the bridge, the eyebar, over sixty-three feet in length and weighing over 5,000 pounds, is at joint C13N and the first link of the chain suspension, about 50 feet west of the Ohio tower. The fractured eyebar is discovered less than 100 feet upstream of the collapse. Upon hearing the news, the mud-covered piece is washed and coated with hair spray to preserve the fracture site.

Tuesday, December 19
(Day 5)

The bodies of a middle-aged woman, a man, and a young child recovered the day before have been identified as James Meadows, his stepson, Timothy, and James' mother-in-law, Alma Duff. The last of the six recovered bodies are Lillian Wedge, Charles Smith, and his wife, Oma. The toll of identified bodies currently stands at 18 (Blackman, Cantrell, Counts, Cremeens, Duff, Lane, Mayes, McManus, Meadows, Meadows, Nibert, Northup, Smith, Smith, Towe, Turner, Wedge, and Wedge), with one unidentified. As many as 40 are said to be missing or unaccounted for.

The funeral service for Gerald McManus is scheduled to begin at 10:30am at the Brock Funeral Home in Portsmouth, Ohio. Burial will follow in South Webster, Ohio.

With daytime temperatures reaching the low 60s, a Chevrolet with West Virginia tags is recovered immediately west of the Ohio tower around 12:30pm. There are no occupants in the car, but the body of a middle-aged male, possibly in his 40s, is discovered nearby. Less than an hour later, a second body is recovered. A male in his early 40s is located not far from the previous body. The second body is discovered in a 1956 Chevrolet bearing Ohio license plates. Both male bodies are removed from the 44-degree water, tagged, and taken to the National Guard Armory for identification. By mid-afternoon, both Paul Scott and Howard Boggs have been released from Pleasant Valley Hospital. Scott returns to his home in Middleport, while Boggs returns to an empty house in Bidwell, having lost his wife and their son in the collapse. It isn't long before Boggs begins showing up at the river's edge, vowing to be there each day until his wife and son are found.

As over thirty-five newspapers across the U.S. continue to share the tragic news of the bridge's collapse, a "B" shift diver reports visibility of approximately one foot or less in the river. Working east of the Ohio tower, the divers find aluminum siding from a truck, part of a baseboard heater, a pack of cigarettes, broken wooden crates, and an air filter from a car.

Funeral services will be held today for a second person from the area to pass away from the bridge's collapse. A remembrance service for Darius Northup is held at Jordan Baptist Church in Gallipolis Ferry. Rev. Odell Bush and Rev. Charles Kinniard will preside, and interment will follow at Wyoma Cemetery in Mason County.

Commuter rail service on the New York Central Railroad begins between Point Pleasant and the Ohio side of the river. On loan from its daily runs between Cincinnati and Cleveland, the train will operate 12 hours a day, five days a week. It will depart Gallipolis on the even hours, beginning at 6:00am, and Point Pleasant on the opposite side of the river on the odd hours. The 30-minute ride includes a stop in Kanauga and will run twice every hour during rush hour. Passengers can ride the train for a one-way fee of 35 cents between Kanauga and Point Pleasant and 50 cents between Point Pleasant and Gallipolis, four miles south of Kanauga. Called the "Doodlebug" car, there is a 75-passenger limit on the train, made fuller by people on both sides of the river traveling to work. Packed like sardines because of limited seats, many of those using the train service during the day are women and teenagers carrying cameras. Thought to be at the time one of the longest trestles in the U.S. and with a middle span of nearly 450 feet, the train's route over the Ohio River provides an excellent view of the salvage operations. Although regular passenger service on the trestle stopped 16 years earlier, train stations already exist on either side of the train bridge. The line is still used by freight trains, so trains will share the railroad bridge located upstream from the wreckage. Commuter train service will most likely stop when ferry service begins.

Hearings conducted by the West Virginia Public Service Commission are set to begin two days after Christmas. The commission is expected to act on applications from companies seeking to start ferry service between Gallipolis and Point Pleasant.

With Christmas less than one week away, many professional workers head home for the holidays. Subsequently, the daily number of workers on the site slowly decreases. Newspaper reporters, photographers, and tv crews also begin to exit the area to follow other news stories.

Apart from the local recovery effort, the collapse of the Silver Bridge prompts a national response. Four days after the disaster, Senator Jennings Randolph of West Virginia, Chairman of the Senate Committee on Public Works, initiates hearings on the matter.

Before the day's end, Mrs. Madge Byus, grandmother of Kathy Byus, shows up at Ordnance Elementary School. She has traveled to the school to clean out the desk and collect her granddaughter's belongings. Kathy's body is one of the more than three dozen bodies yet to be recovered. As she collects Kathy's belongings, it is said that Mrs. Byus' crying quickly brings the school's teachers and staff to tears.

As morning temperatures in the low 30s give way to afternoon temperatures in the low 60s, two more names are added to the list of bodies identified. The names of James White and Marvin Wamsley bring the current list of deceased to 20, although one body remains unidentified. Estimates remain of upwards of 30 still missing or unaccounted for.

A diver from the "A" shift reports he has arrived near the center of the middle span and discovers a heavy concentration of vehicles, possibly as many as eight or more. Initially, a "B" shift diver reports recovering a car muffler. He can also see part of the roadway deck of the bridge sitting on top of a late model Ford with Ohio plates. As the diver hooks onto the car and attempts to have it lifted to the surface by the crane, the vehicle gets caught on the cab of a tractor-trailer. The diver notes the lettering on the door of the tractor-trailer…NC ICC 128-131. After hooking onto the tractor-trailer's cab, the cab is lifted to the surface around 9:00am. Initially, authorities on the surface find only one body in the cab of the Roadway tractor-trailer, a male in his late 20s or early 30s. A second male body in his mid to late 20s is discovered several minutes later in the rear of the cab. The bodies are immediately tagged and transported to the armory in Point Pleasant. Meanwhile, the late-model Ford remains on the bottom of the river.

Just before 12:00noon, divers locate a Ford with West Virginia tags near the center of the middle span. Painted on the door of the car are the words Pickens Cab Company. After the car's location is noted, the vehicle is lifted to the surface. The authorities find the bodies of two males inside. One body is that of a middle-aged man, while the second body is a much younger man. The young man is holding a $1 bill between his thumb and forefinger. The two bodies are tagged and sent on to the coroner. Just after 1:00pm, a fifth body is recovered inside a Ford with an Ohio license plate. Containing the body of a young male, the car is recovered south of the center of the

88

middle span.

About the same time the last of the four bodies is recovered, the first of no less than eleven funerals are scheduled. The funeral for Alma Duff is expected to begin at 9:30am in the chapel of the Crow-Hussell Funeral Home. The Rev. Landis Absten will officiate, and the burial will be in Mount Flower Cemetery near Leon, West Virginia. A remembrance service will be held for Vic Turner at 10:00am at the Gospel Tabernacle in Point Pleasant, with burial to follow at Suncrest Cemetery. Turner would have celebrated a birthday on January 22nd. A joint funeral service for Duff's son-in-law and grandson, James Meadows, and his son, Timothy, will take place in the chapel of the Crow-Hussell Funeral Home beginning at 12:00noon. Rev. Landis Absten will officiate, and burial will follow at Buffalo Memorial Park in Putnam County, West Virginia. This will be Absten's second funeral of the day.

The funeral service for Donald Cremeens begins at 12:30pm at the Poplar Ridge Church near Kyger. The Rev. John Jeffers will preside, and burial will follow at Poplar Ridge Cemetery. There are two funeral services planned for 2:00pm. The funeral service for the unidentified female, now known to be Maxine Sturgeon, will be held in the chapel at the Mohr-Stevens Funeral Home in Point Pleasant, with Rev. Norman Nash officiating. Burial to follow at Beech Hill Cemetery near Southside. At the same time, the service for Nora Nibert is scheduled at Beale Methodist Church in Apple Grove. Burial will follow in the church cemetery with Rev. Odell Bush officiating. This will be Rev. Bush's second funeral in as many days. Also taking place at 2:00pm is the funeral for Darlene Mayes. Her service will be at the Church of Christ in Christian Union in Gallipolis. Burial will be in the Henderson Cemetery.

At 3:00pm, two funerals are scheduled to take place. The funeral service for Alva Lane will be held at the McCoy-Wetherholt Funeral Home in Gallipolis beginning at 3:00pm. The Rev. Everett Delaney will preside, and interment will follow at Maddy Cemetery near Addison. A joint funeral service for Paul and Lillian Wedge will occur in the Crow-

Hussell Funeral Home chapel. Officiating at the service are Rev. Charles Frum and Rev. Charles A. Pitzer. Burial will follow at Kirkland Memorial Gardens in Point Pleasant.

More than 250 members of the Boilermakers Union 687, working at the Ft. Marion Power Plant, are idle today in respect of Paul Wedge. In lieu of flowers, the children of Paul and Lillian Wedge ask that donations be made to the Paul and Lillian Wedge Scholarship Fund established at the Citizens National Bank in Point Pleasant. Over 400 people attend the Wedge funeral, including members of the boys' basketball team at Point Pleasant High School, where son Jimmy Joe Wedge is the head coach.

As the body of Darlene Mayes is carried from the church, six of her female classmates at Gallia Academy Junior High School line the walkway. While several of Deenie's female classmates hold a flower as her body makes its way from the church, one of the male classmates at the school, David Chapman, the younger brother of bridge survivor, Judy Chapman, serves as a pallbearer. Darlene is buried on her mother's birthday and one day after her father's birthday, and she would have turned 14 on January 14th. In addition, Darlene is buried with a pair of horseshoes that would have been a Christmas gift for her.

Although barge traffic is open for boats on the Kanawha River headed south on the Ohio River, it is not the case for tugboats wishing to head north on the Ohio. There are currently no less than five tugboats tied-up on the Kanawha waiting to make the northward trip. This includes the A.V. Criss owned by Atlas Towing Company, moored on the north side of the river. Other tugboats mooring on the Kanawha are the Jefferson owned by River Transportation Inc. and two boats owned by the Bulk Towing Company, the H. E. Bowles and the Beaver. One boat on the Kanawha reports it has been waiting almost four days. As for the tugboats pushing barges stopped on the Ohio, it is no different.

Between miles 262 and 267 on the river, around 30 tugboats on both sides of the wreckage are waiting their turn to proceed. Among those waiting are three boats owned by the Ohio River Company, the John J. Rowe waiting downstream, and the Tibolt and the Walter Beckjord upstream. Combined, these three tugboats alone are pushing nearly fifty barges and have been waiting a collective 10 days. The Humble Oil and Refining Company has two boats waiting upstream of the bridge site, and the same stands true for the Point Towing Company. The Ohio Barge Line Inc. has boats waiting on opposite sides of the wreckage. The Steel Pioneer is tied up south of the site on the West Virginia shore, while a sister boat, the Steel Clipper, is moored upstream of the site. The Harvey Jordan, owned by U.S. Steel and under the command of tugboat Captain Jones, has been waiting for nearly six days south of the Kanawha with its six barges of coal.

Moreover, eight tugboats mooring south of the former bridge are hauling materials in excess of sixty tons each. Upstream, the twenty boats that line the western shoreline and the nine tugs tied-up on the West Virginia side make the Ohio River's width appear strikingly narrow. It is estimated that over three hundred and seventy-five barges are mooring at some point on the river, and over two hundred are loaded.

The citizens of Huntington displayed their compassion for those affected by the collapse. Food for the families and toys for the children are collected, in addition to cash. A portion of all that's collected is given to the First Presbyterian Church in Point Pleasant. At the same time, an equal amount is delivered to Grace Methodist Church in Gallipolis.

It is reported that most drivers using the bridges in the immediate area are taking it extremely slow. The drivers are spacing themselves as much as 100 feet or more behind the vehicles ahead. Consequently, this has resulted in slower traffic crossing the bridges and some reports of minor congestion.

Four additional bodies are recovered as the remaining crews work into the afternoon and evening. The first body, a young male, is recovered from the inside of a Rambler near the center of the middle span. A second body, a female in her late 20s, is found outside of a 1956 Chevrolet near the west tower.

The latter body is located as workers use a new type of sonar brought in earlier that afternoon. A grappling hook brings the body to the surface. After removing the cab of a tractor-trailer lifted to the surface earlier, a third body is recovered around 9:00pm in a Ford bearing Ohio tags. As the late model Ford discovered earlier is brought to the surface, divers report no additional bodies inside.

Just before midnight, a body is recovered from the inside of a gravel truck located just east of the center of the middle span. It takes several hours to lift the bridge's steel off the 6-ton vehicle before the body can be hauled to the surface. Each of the last two vehicles contains a male in their late 20s or early 30s. The eight bodies recovered this day are the largest number recovered on one day since operations began three days earlier.

As more and more vehicles are recovered and bodies removed, workers begin removing parts of the bridge's superstructure from the site. Blasting is used to break up bridge iron structures but intermittently not to scare local people. As parts of the fallen bridge are placed into barges, the barges quickly fill up. Meanwhile, the West Virginia State Road Commission begins to explore a site south of the former bridge site for all bridge wreckage collected by the Corps. of Engineers. In time, the bridge parts will be reassembled to hopefully discover the cause of the collapse. All recovered vehicles are taken to an area north of Point Pleasant, near the Marietta Manufacturing facility. The cranes used to remove cars, bodies, and parts of the bridge are invaluable, and the $4,000 a day cost to rent the cranes seems insignificant.

In Washington, DC, President Lyndon Johnson directs the National Transportation Safety Board (NTSB) to investigate the bridge's collapse and determine the cause. The action comes one year after the Highway Safety Act (1966) and includes a provision for the Department of Transportation to establish a formalized program for bridge inspections. Subsequently, three separate committees or working groups are appointed. First, there is a bridge design review and history group headed by W. J. Wilkes. Assisting Wilkes will be the commissioner of the West Virginia State Road Commission, a representative from the Ohio Department of Highways, and Frank Masters of the Modjeski and Masters engineering firm of Harrisburg, Pennsylvania. A second group, the witness interrogation group, will be chaired by Anthony Schmeig and include a member of the West Virginia State Police, the Ohio State Highway Patrol, and a member from Modjeski and Masters. Charles Scheffey will lead the third group, the structural analysis and test group. In addition to its own technicians, the structural analysis and test group will be supplemented by technical representatives from all parties of interest, including representatives from West Virginia and Ohio, the J. E. Greiner Company, and members from U. S. Steel, the parent company of the builders of the superstructure, the American Bridge Company.

As the world learns of the passing of Louis Washansky, the first person to receive a human heart transplant, the chalk blackboard at the Point Pleasant Courthouse is updated and includes eight new names. Today's list of deceased are identified as Julius Bennett, Gene Mabe, Leo Sanders, Ronnie Moore, James Maxwell, Donna Casey, James Hawkins, and Forrest Higley. Julius Bennett, the first name appearing on the list, celebrated his birthday eight days before passing away. This brings the current total of deceased from the Silver Bridge collapse at the start of the day to 29 (Bennett, Blackman, Cantrell, Casey, Counts, Cremeens, Duff, Hawkins, Higley, Lane, Mabe, Maxwell, Mayes, McManus, Meadows, Meadows, Moore, Nibert, Northup, Sanders, Smith, Smith, Sturgeon, Towe, Turner, Wamsley, Wedge, Wedge, and White). Meanwhile, authorities adjust the list of missing or unaccounted for to around 25.

As a result of the dams upstream not allowing as much water to be released, an "A" shift diver reports the current is less than it has been in previous days. Moving east toward the West Virginia tower, the divers come across a Chevrolet bearing Ohio plates. After hooking on to the car and having it lifted to the shore by the crane, the body of a middle-aged male is discovered inside. Just before 10:00am, two members of the Orrville (Ohio) Divemasters Recovery Team come across a late model Ford Mustang located near the center of the bridge's middle span. The vehicle is brought to the surface after authorities note the car's location and model. Inside are two bodies, a young woman, possibly in her late 20s or early 30s, and a young child. A third body, a school-aged female, is believed to have been in the car at the time of the collapse. The presence of the Orrville dive team may have been part of the recovery operations because of the relationship that one of the divers of the team, Francis Berkey, had with the Mason County coroner at the time, Dr. Eschenaur. Before arriving in the Point

Pleasant area, Dr. Eschenaur had a medical practice in Orrville, and Berkey was one of his patients.

As with the day before, several funerals are planned for this day. The funeral for Marvin Wamsley will be held in the chapel of Crow-Hussell Funeral home, beginning at 11:00am. Officiating the service will be W. A. Wilcoxen and burial will follow at Suncrest Cemetery in Point Pleasant. Point Pleasant High School teacher and coach James White's funeral will occur in the Honaker-Harris chapel in Logan, West Virginia, beginning at 2:00pm. The Rev. Gaston Boyle will preside, and burial will follow at Forest Lawn Cemetery in Pecks Mills, West Virginia. A remembrance service for Roadway Express driver Gene Mabe is planned for 4:00pm in the chapel of Sechrest Funeral Home. The Rev. J. E. Nelson and Elder Charles Pichard will officiate, and burial will follow at Guilford Memorial Park Cemetery in Greensboro, North Carolina.

With daytime temperatures reaching the low 70s, cranes continue removing steel from both sides of the river. Divers report that 75% of the wreckage has been surveyed. Subsequently, search teams on the river will widen their search area, moving south toward the mouth of the Kanawha River and beyond. Twenty-four vehicles have been recovered, including eighteen cars, four tractor-trailers, one gravel truck, and one pickup.

Merchants on both sides of the river take note of a growing phenomenon. There seems to be a sudden demand for picture postcards showing the Silver Bridge before its collapse.

Around 9:00pm, tugboat captains receive word that a single lane through a nearly 250-foot wide channel in the river has been reopened for barge traffic. Tugboats and barges must have a draw of fewer than 13½ feet. Additionally, boats must have special spotting crews looking out for bodies, and the captains are told that their passage may be halted at any time due to salvage work.

It is said that the first tugboat to pass the site may have been the National, owned by the Elk Towing Company, pushing eight barges loaded with coal and four empty ones. The next to pass through the collapse site is the Sarah Jane, owned by Thomas Petroleum, hauling petroleum. Col. Falck is quick to respond when asked why the Sarah Jane is not allowed to pass first since it has been moored closest to the collapse site. "If there was an obstacle that escaped detention, I preferred it ripped open a coal-laden barge rather than one loaded with petroleum" (*The Herald-Dispatch*). The third boat to pass the steel remains of the bridge may have been the Polly R, owned by B & B Towing. It is pushing four empty barges. As it progresses through the site, high winds push the vessel and its barges into the boat where Falck is viewing operations. Possibly passing the area shortly after the National, the Sarah Jane and the Polly R. is the George T. Price, owned by River Transportation, Inc., and the W. S. Rhea, owned by Mississippi Valley Barge Line Inc. Both the Price and the Rhea have been moored to the west side of the Ohio for nearly six days.

During the night, thieves burglarize three Point Pleasant businesses as police are preoccupied with patrol duty at the collapse site. One burglary occurs at the Welfare Finance Company located at 415 Main Street. In addition to checks and personal records, a safe containing as much as $1,400 in cash is missing. Entrance into the office is made by a rear door that's been pried open. Police report that a second store, the Point Service Store, half a block away at 400 Main Street, is also burglarized. The business owner says around ten handguns, several shotguns, a rifle, and some knives are among the missing items. Also missing is $25.00. A third business is also hit during the night. The Salem Market, located at 2121 Jackson Street, reports that cash in the amount of around $75.00 and some merchandise are missing. The burglars broke into the store through a basement window. They also cut telephone cables leaving many residents and businesses without phone service.

Friday, December 22
(Day 8)

Despite an on-and-off rain in the area, the temperatures on the first day of winter reach the high 60s. However, high winds and rough waters limit the recovery efforts. The optimism of the 70 or more workers is tempered with the addition of three more names to the chalkboard. Of the 32 deceased individuals identified to date, fifteen are from West Virginia, thirteen are from Ohio, and two each from Virginia and North Carolina. The latest names added to the list of those deceased include Thomas "Bus" Lee, Hilda Byus, and her 2-year-old daughter, Kimberly. The third person in the Byus car, 10-year-old Kathy, remains missing. Adjusted numbers of those possibly missing or unaccounted for have fallen to 19, including Kathy Byus, Denzil Taylor, Glenna Taylor, and Maxine Turner, all from Point Pleasant; Albert Adler, Kristy and Marjorie Boggs, Thomas Cantrell, Alonzo Darst, Robert Head, Frederick Miller, James Pullen, and Ronald Sims, from Ohio; and Harold Cundiff from North Carolina. Also listed as possibly missing are Alvie and Lori Maddox of New York, Betty Street of Honaker, VA, Howard Fisher, and R.R. Simms. At the time, the last two have no known address.

Around 12:00noon, the safe from the Welfare Finance Company office is recovered from the burglaries that happened the night before. The safe is discovered at the Salt Creek garbage dump located south of Point Pleasant along Route 2. Although the safe contains over $500 worth of checks and various records, cash is the only item reported missing. Police believe that it would have taken three or four men to remove the safe from the office, considering the safe measures nearly 4-feet tall, three-feet deep, and almost two-feet wide. A special wrecker is brought in to haul away the safe. Besides the safe, police find four portable radios and a used portable tv reported missing from the burglary at the Point Service Store. Among the items still missing from the Salem Market are over $100 in cash, one case of coffee, several cans of baby food, around 50 cartons of cigarettes, an electric skillet, a toaster, an iron, and a Japanese sword.

Several funerals are scheduled for today, with many beginning at the same time. The funeral for Donna Casey will begin at 1:00pm at the Church of God on Garfield Avenue in Point Pleasant. The Rev. L. M. Foudy will officiate, with burial to follow at Lone Oak Cemetery. She leaves behind a husband and two children. Also beginning at 1:00pm is a service of remembrance for Ronnie Moore. His funeral will occur in the F. L. Stevers Funeral Home chapel in Mercerville, Ohio, with E. C. Delaney officiating. Burial will follow at the Crown City Cemetery.

There are three additional funeral services scheduled for later in the afternoon. At 2:00pm, a joint funeral service for Charles and Oma Smith will be conducted at the First Church of God in Gallipolis, with the Rev. Ezra Bowen and Rev. John Wheeler presiding. The burial will take place at Calvary Cemetery. The funeral for James Maxwell is set for 3:00pm at the Miller Funeral Home. Rev. Everett Delaney will officiate, and burial will follow at Pine Street Cemetery. The funeral for Leo "Doc" Sanders, who would have turned 43 on the day his body is recovered, will occur at the Ida Baptist Church in Bentre, West Virginia. The Rev. Charles Frum will preside, with interment to follow at Elliott Cemetery in Lizemore, West Virginia. The funeral service for Julius Bennett, the third of the Roadway Express Company employees to pass away from the bridge collapse, is scheduled today, 2:00pm, at Bethel Baptist Church in Walnut Cove, North Carolina.

Before dismissal for the Christmas break, a memorial service is held at Point Pleasant High School for teachers James White, who passed away following the bridge collapse, business teacher Denzil Taylor, and his pregnant wife, Glenna. The bodies of the Taylors have yet to be recovered.

Local authorities on both sides of the Ohio warn people to be careful. It seems that scammers are phoning residents and soliciting funds to assist in the work to find any additional victims.

The recovery and salvage operations continue 24 hours a day, seven days a week, and there have been no reported injuries. However, it could be that many of the local workers remember what happened on this day fourteen years ago at the Marietta Manufacturing Plant when 8 men died from an explosion. Since the river has been reopened for barge traffic, there have been nearly 25 barges a day passing the site of the fallen bridge.

Saturday, December 23
(Day 9)

With a river temperature around 45 degrees, wind, and the mid-morning temperature outside hovering in the low 20s, authorities report that no additional bodies have been recovered. The total confirmed remains at 32. However, the number of possible missing persons has been revised to 14, including Albert Adler, Marjorie Boggs, Kimberly Boggs, Kathy Byus, Thomas Cantrell, Harold Cundiff, Alonzo Darst, Robert Head, Frederick Miller, James Pullen, Ronald Sims, Denzil Taylor, Glenna Taylor, and Maxine Turner. Overnight, five names are removed from the list of missing or unaccounted for, including Alvie and Lori Maddox, and Betty Street. A fourth person on the missing list, Howard Fisher, has been identified as John Fishel of Petersburg, Virginia, who survived the collapse. The last missing person identified as R. R. Simms is Ronald Sims of Gallipolis, Ohio. With no other bodies recovered after two days, the recovery efforts shifted to the West Virginia side of the river.

The funeral for Thomas "Bus" Lee is scheduled at 2:00pm at the Waugh-Halley-Wood Funeral Home in Gallipolis. The Rev. Albert McGee is officiating, and burial will follow at Pine Street Cemetery in Gallipolis.

With the sub-freezing temperatures in the areas, authorities are also asking for donations of small portable heaters to be used in the smaller search boats. Negotiations are underway for the engineering firm of Modjeski and Masters to inspect bridges at Parkersburg and New Martinsville. Additionally, the firm has also been hired to inspect three Ohio-maintained bridges spanning the Ohio River: the Pomeroy-Mason Bridge, the Chester/Newell-East Liverpool Bridge, and Ft. Steuben Bridge Steubenville. Ohio authorities have allocated $40,000 for the inspections.

Beyond the announcement that estimated expenses for the first week of operations are around $100,000, the West Virginia State Road Commission shares that wreckage from the bridge will begin to be reassembled on a 25-acre piece of pasture south of Point Pleasant. Garland Steele, with the West Virginia Department of Highways, will work with the forensics team to reassemble the bridge in hopes of finding what caused it to fail.

With the thoughts of the collapse still fresh on the minds of most residents, a negative mood remains on both sides of the river. Many residents admit they don't feel like shopping, and when asked about the swollen faces and red eyes, most blame it on a cold or the windy weather. Moreover, the Point Pleasant Ministerial Association is inviting all churches in the area to observe a period of silence during Christmas Eve services planned for tomorrow evening. Ministers ask that people pray for the workers and those who have lost loved ones.

With the recovery efforts into their second full week, the news surrounding the bridge's collapse seems to be falling from the front pages of many newspapers. Exactly one week after the tragedy, over sixty newspapers in twenty states are still reporting on events at the site. By December 24, the number of newspapers that run an article about the collapse has decreased to 40 newspapers in thirteen states.

The talk around both sides of the Ohio was that "silent night" came early this year, and it is said that no Christmas music was played in local stores for several days. But when words like "glad to see you" are exchanged on the street or in the grocery line, they come from the heart and mean something.

Divers from Marine Contracting Incorporated continue the grim task of recovering cars and bodies. Two vehicles are recovered today, a late-model Pontiac and a late-model Volkswagen, and both have Ohio license plates. However, divers report the cars do not contain bodies. The last time a body was recovered is three days ago, on December 21. The current number of vehicles recovered now stands at twenty-six, including twenty cars, four tractor-trailers, one gravel truck, and one pickup.

A toy drive by the city of Huntington has been completed. The toys will be delivered to children who lost a parent in the bridge collapse.

The West Virginia State Road Commission has reached a verbal agreement with the Henderson landowners to rent land where the bridge can be reassembled. However, the owners refuse to sign a contract. The State Road Commission offers $250 a month for a one-year lease, while the owners seek $8,000 a month. A judge will decide on a fair price in the next few weeks.

Around 9:30pm, the body of a middle-aged male is

recovered by divers outside of a late model Dodge with Ohio plates. After the automobile is brought to the surface and the lone body is removed, the body is then transferred to the Coast Guard boat, tagged, and sent to the coroner.

Monday, December 25
(Day 11)

As temperatures take more than a 40-degree drop in less than 24 hours, from 71 degrees on Christmas Eve to 30 degrees on Christmas Day, the body recovered yesterday has been positively identified as that of Robert Head. The automobile of Head was brought to the surface last week; however, his body was not in his car. The death toll from the bridge collapse now stands at 33, with 13 still missing. Another body has also been recovered that's not related to the bridge's collapse ten days earlier.

Around 10:00am, recovery workers discover the body of a middle-aged male approximately one mile east of the confluence of the Kanawha River and the Ohio. The body is identified as Robert Rodgers of Racine, Ohio. He was a deckhand with the Tri-State Material Company of Parkersburg and fell into the Kanawha River near Arbuckle, West Virginia, on November 14.

Despite the holiday, the work continues in the recovery efforts. Around lunchtime, workers are served a Christmas dinner prepared by Lambda Chi Omega sorority members, the Red Cross, and the Salvation Army. It is said that Col. William Falck and his wife eat their Christmas dinner aboard one of the local tugboats. Considering the time and energy that Civil Defense Director John (Andy) Wilson has devoted to search and recovery since the disaster, volunteers threatened to quit if Wilson does not go home and spend time with his family.

At the close of the day, authorities announce that they are seeking witnesses who may have seen or been near the bridge on the day of the collapse. In like manner, authorities report that a second Merry Stone Company dump truck is recovered and lifted to the surface. However, unlike the first Merry Stone truck recovered five days earlier, no bodies are discovered in the second truck. It is also being reported that the Hennis Freight Lines tractor-trailer has been recovered. No bodies are found in the cab. With this recovery, the five tractor-trailers on the bridge at the time of collapse have all been found. The body of Hennis employee Harold Cundiff remains missing.

Tuesday, December 26
(Day 12)

On the same day that Bob Hope and his entourage of Ann Margaret and Miss World, Madeleine Hartog Bell, are entertaining U.S. troops stationed in Pleiku, South Vietnam, divers prepare to lift to the surface the late-model Dodge discovered on Christmas Eve. As they do so, the divers come across two bodies from the site of the bridge's collapse that may have been overlooked prior. The first body is a middle-aged male and was brought to the surface around 3:00am. The second body, also a middle-aged male, is recovered approximately 30-minutes later.

A joint funeral service for Hilda Byus, and her 2-year-old daughter, Kimberly, will take place at the First Baptist Church in Point Pleasant beginning at 2:00pm. The Rev. Ted Wall will officiate, and burial will follow at Concord Cemetery. A second daughter, Kathy Byus, age 10, remains missing. The last two bodies are the thirty-fourth, and thirty-fifth recovered to date.

At a press briefing, the West Virginia State Road Commission confirms that a maintenance engineer from District I made a visual inspection of the Silver Bridge earlier in the year. In his report, the engineer says nothing about any damages or potential damages to the bridge. One SRC supervisor believes the failure is not in the deck but may lie with a weakness in the steel eyebars. With today's recovery, local authorities report that twenty-nine vehicles have been retrieved, including twenty-one cars, five tractor-trailers, two gravel trucks, and one pickup. Sources say that two vehicles are yet to be recovered, a Ford belonging to Denzil and Glenna Taylor and a late model Chevrolet belonging to Howard and Marjorie Boggs. The number of missing persons remains at thirteen.

Interviews begin for anyone that may have seen or been near the bridge at the time of the collapse. As investigators near the end of the questioning process, they report nearly 150

106

persons have been interviewed, and over one-half have given statements. The interviews bring a myriad of different stories. Some witnesses say the bridge collapse happened before 5:00pm, while others say it happened after 5:00pm. Several witnesses say the bridge was gone in a matter of seconds. At the same time, others testify that the total collapse took anywhere from 30 seconds to a full minute. Last but not least, some witnesses report seeing anywhere from 50 to 75 cars on the bridge. Conversely, other witnesses say that it was about half that number.

Officials project that it may take as long as eight months or more to reconstruct the old bridge. Other leaders say the reassembling process could take longer than it did to build the bridge. Meanwhile, the cost to construct a new, two-lane bridge is estimated between $4,000,000 and $6,000,000. A new four-lane bridge to span the Ohio River between Point Pleasant and Gallipolis is projected to cost in the range of $9,000,000. To date, the Corps. of Engineers reports they have removed over 1,300 tons of steel from the river. Moreover, the Corps. anticipates that the job can be completed in a week or so with good weather.

Wednesday, December 27
(Day 13)

The additional names appearing on the chalk blackboard located at the Point Pleasant Courthouse are Frederick Miller and James Pullen. Miller and Pullen were riding in a car along with Paul Scott; however, Scott is the only one of the three to survive. The list of deceased currently stands at 35, with eleven still missing.

But no sooner had word gotten out in the communities that the two bodies recovered were those of Pullen and Miller, a 36th body from the collapse is recovered. A few hours before daybreak, a pregnant female's body in her early 20s is found along with a late model Ford Fairlane bearing West Virginia plates. The body is discovered, tangled in steel and about 40 feet beneath the surface by workers dragging the river. Also recovered among the twisted steel is a late-model Ford Falcon station wagon. The divers report not seeing any other bodies inside the car. As the last of the divers depart, the total number of recovered vehicles is now thirty-four.

The widow of Melvin Cantrell, Margaret Cantrell, is involved in a car accident. A passenger in the car, 8-year-old son Terry Cantrell, is injured and receives eight stitches in his hand and nearly three dozen around his face. Mrs. Cantrell has scratches around the face and a black eye. The truck the Cantrells are riding in, which contains groceries and donated toys, is demolished. It is believed that none of the other Cantrell children are in the vehicle at the time of the accident. Mr. Cantrell's body is one of the first bodies recovered on December 15.

As they seek approval from the Interstate Commerce Commission and the Army Corps. of Engineers, the West Virginia Public Service Commission has received word that one of the three applicants desiring to operate a ferry between Point Pleasant and Kanauga, the Ferry Service Inc. of Point Pleasant, has withdrawn their name from consideration. The two companies still in the running for the service are the

Appalachian Company of Lexington, Kentucky, and the Ohio Valley Towing out of Glenwillard, Pennsylvania. A final decision on who will be awarded the ferry contract will be announced sometime during the first week of January.

The Corps. of Engineers estimates that the search and recovery efforts have cost between $100,000 and $125,000. Renting the derricks and towboats is around $5,000 a day.

Following visitation at the Waugh-Halley-Wood Funeral Home, the body of Robert (Bobby) Head will be driven to the Challo Funeral home in Chattanooga, Tennessee. Burial will follow at the National Cemetery.

Thursday, December 28
(Day 14)

The lone body recovered yesterday has been identified as Glenna Mae Taylor. To date, the body of her husband, Denzil, has not been recovered. The total number of recovered bodies from the bridge collapse stands at 36, with ten people still missing.

There are two funerals scheduled for today. The funeral for Frederick Miller is expected to begin at 1:00pm at Waugh-Halley-Wood Funeral Home. Rev. Ronald Justice will officiate, and burial will follow at Mound Hill Cemetery. Miller leaves behind a wife and two children, ages 2 and 4. The funeral service for James Pullen will begin at 3:00pm at the Rawlings-Coates Funeral Home in Middleport, Ohio. Rev. Charles Simon will preside, and burial will follow in Riverview Cemetery.

Despite 4 inches of snow, the work of recovery and salvage continues. Authorities report that 75% of the wreckage is now in the salvage yard in Henderson. Meanwhile, several National Transportation Safety Board members have planned a follow-up inspection of the St. Marys Bridge.

The Veterans Administration asks the communities on both sides of the river for the names of veterans who passed away from the bridge collapse. The Silver Bridge Disaster Fund Committee announces that the fund amount now stands at nearly $3,000, with the money to be distributed among the families that lost loved ones in the collapse.

The Civil Defense reports that their general operations will cease in the next few days since the emergency is over. Except for a few minor jobs such as operations and communications, all other duties will be turned over to the Corps. of Engineers, the Coast Guard, and the West Virginia State Police by midnight on December 31. In addition, the temporary morgue at the National Guard Armory in Point Pleasant will be closed at 3:00pm. Henceforth, any bodies recovered will be taken to a funeral home for proper identification.

Friday, December 29
(Day 15)

While no bodies have been recovered since Wednesday, December 27, the public is reminded of those ten persons whose bodies are yet to be recovered. The list of missing includes Albert Adler, Kristy and Marjorie Boggs, Kathy Byus, Thomas Cantrell, Harold Cundiff, Lonzo Darst, Ronald Sims, Denzil Taylor, and Maxine Turner.

Although the first significant snowfall followed by a dense fog may have temporarily slowed recovery efforts, the business of recovery and salvage continues. The Coast Guard vessel Poplar from Sewickley, Pennsylvania, with a crew of 20, arrived a few days earlier to assist in the recovery efforts. It relieves the vessel, Oleander, which has been at the site for nearly two weeks. The Coast Guard also reports that since the site was opened for barge traffic on December 22, almost two dozen towboats a day pass the location of the fallen bridge.

As with so many other groups that offered aid and assistance and whose services are no longer needed, Trinity Methodist Church in Gallipolis has announced their food canteen will be shutting down at the end of the day. On the opposite shore is the food truck of the Salvation Army. It, too, has been shut down since it is no longer needed. Except for those in communications and operations, all the Civil Defense personnel has been released.

It was announced that the first press briefing probing the collapse will occur tomorrow, December 30. Meanwhile, local authorities have determined that only one vehicle, a late model Chevrolet, remains to be recovered. The car is owned by Howard Boggs and may contain his wife's and young daughter's bodies. Furthermore, officials believe that all remaining bodies will likely be found outside their vehicles if more cars are recovered.

Saturday, December 30
(Day 16)

Not long after the morning press conference begins, authorities announce they are looking at around 10 possible causes of the bridge's collapse. The causes being explored include bridge overload, old age, wind, vibrations, design failure, metal fatigue, anchorage failure, and suspension system failure, particularly the eyebars. Officials also report that contacting any additional witnesses is proving difficult since the remaining eyewitnesses do not live in either West Virginia or Ohio.

The body of Glenna Taylor is taken to Lewis-Rogers Funeral Home in Pennsboro, West Virginia. Mrs. Taylor's funeral will be held today at 2:00pm in the funeral home chapel. Should the body of her husband, Denzil, be recovered before the service, a joint funeral service will be held. Burial will be at the International Order of Odd Fellows Cemetery in Harrisville, West Virginia.

There is little doubt that the top news story in the state of West Virginia for 1967 is the bridge collapse. In a distant second are the spring floods, which hit the Weston and Glenville areas of the state and caused more than $2,000,000 in damage. The number three news item of the year involves the Marine from Nitro who killed two Vietnamese civilians. Rounding out the top 5 news stories in the state is the entrapment of a youth in a well for 24 hours in Williamson, Mingo County, and the derailment of a Baltimore and Ohio train near Pennsboro that killed two. Finally, the number seven top story of 1967 is the Fairmont State College Falcons and their NAIA small college national football championship.

Sunday, December 31
(Day 17)

Despite a heavy fog that reduces recovery operations on the river, the Coast Guard continues to make two runs daily between the former bridge site and the Gallipolis Dam to search for bodies. On both sides of the Ohio, flags still fly at half-staff for the thirty-six deceased persons and the ten missing ones.

Around mid-day, one of the last survivors hospitalized in the collapse, William Edmondson, is released from Pleasant Valley Hospital in Point Pleasant.

Up to this point, thirty of the thirty-one vehicles reported to have been on the bridge at the time of the collapse have been recovered. This includes twenty-two cars: seven Fords, five Chevrolets, four Pontiacs, two Ramblers, a Buick, a Dodge, an Oldsmobile, and a Volkswagen. In addition, two Roadway tractor-trailers, a McLean, a Transcon, and a Hennis semi, have been recovered. The last of the thirty vehicles recovered are two gravel trucks and a pickup.

As the seventeen days following the collapse progressed, the news surrounding the tragic event seems to fall from the front page of most newspapers. If an article does appear regarding the collapse, it seems almost in the sense of passing or filling extra space. On December 16, the story of the bridge's collapse appeared in no less than one hundred fifty newspapers nationally and internationally. One week later, news surrounding the collapse has decreased to just over sixty newspapers in over twenty states. On December 29, information about the collapse and its aftermath appear in approximately ten newspapers nationwide. By year's end, if any newspapers nationwide are still printing anything about the collapse, it was only a paragraph or two on the last page. Far and above, the most loyal newspapers to stay with the story are the local and regional ones, like the *Athens Messenger* (Ohio), *Charleston Daily Mail*, the *Charleston Gazette*, the (Huntington) *Herald-Dispatch*, the *Herald-Advertiser,* the

Daily Sentinel (Meigs County, Ohio), and the *Point Pleasant Register*.

With much of the fallen bridge recovered and transported to the site in Henderson, the last operational offices set up to oversee rescue and recovery begin to close for good around sunset. As for the remainder that are still operating after 6:00pm, most plan to close their offices at midnight. A progress report is expected in 30 days, and a final report from the NTSB is anticipated in 6 months. As authorities announce that all steel from the bridge will be out of the Ohio River by mid-January, the two derrick boats from the Dravo Corporation are released from their duties and begin making their way upriver to Racine.

Mason County officials have been told that since the Silver Bridge was located in their county, local leaders need to add the number of persons killed when the bridge collapsed to their year-end total of people killed on its highways. This will increase the county's recorded deaths from 11 to 42, a whopping increase of nearly 375% from the original number. Likewise, Gallia County has been told to add the five persons killed on the Ohio side of the bridge to their numbers.

The Year 1968

As the calendar flips from 1967 to 1968, the last of federally-funded groups, the Corps. of Engineers, officially ends operations at the site at midnight the night before. Like so many other groups that have left the area, the Corps. feels that its main focus is done since most of the bridge's steel has been moved to the salvage site in Henderson. Similarly, the river's channel is fully open now from its prior width of two hundred fifty feet. In addition, the large derrick boats and the clamshell cranes have left the scene, along with several workboats. However, the Coast Guard remains.

A Corps. report is given with some detail regarding those persons and the vehicles on the bridge at the time of the collapse. It is reported that there were thirty-seven vehicles on the bridge at the time of the failure on Friday evening, December 15, 1967. Of that number, twenty-four went into the waters of the Ohio River and seven vehicles dropped onto the Ohio bank (Fowler, McCleese, Hayman, McLean Trucking, Cantrell, McManus, and Transcon Trucking). The seven vehicles that did not go into the water contained eighteen persons and four casualties (Blackman, M. Cantrell, Counts, McManus). A total of nine persons are rescued and taken to area hospitals (Boggs, Cantrell, Edmundson, Ellis, Fishel, Needham, Nunn, Scott, and F. Wamsley). There have been thirty-six bodies recovered to date, and ten remain missing. The Corps. estimates that nearly 1,350 tons of steel were removed from the river, including the middle and West Virginia span and parts of the Ohio span.

As the first week of the new year nears its end, the state of West Virginia announces they are assuming full responsibility for operations at the site of the fallen bridge. Meanwhile, the last significant portions of the bridge are recovered and taken to Henderson to be reassembled with other parts. The estimated search, recovery, and salvage cost during the past three weeks is over $150,000. This does not include overtime pay for law enforcement and rescue workers.

As welders on the Ohio shore use a cutting torch to free a truck containing hazardous materials, a fire breaks out.

116

Members of the Coast Guard vessel Poplar are called from their water duties to fight the fire on the Ohio shore. The truck has been pinned under the bridge's wreckage since the collapse on December 15. At about the same time, a car located at the far west end of the bridge is being prepared for transport to a waiting barge. The car was partially crushed by a falling light post at the collapse.

The following day it is announced that a representative from the Office of Veterans Affairs will be at the Libby Hotel in Gallipolis to discuss claims of veterans who lost their lives in the bridge collapse. While many of the families have made claims, the representative has yet to be contacted by the families of Robert Head, Thomas Lee, and James White.

With most professional workers no longer on-site, volunteers have taken over dragging operations. Local leaders on the West Virginia side of the river plead for those interested in assisting with the dragging operations to show up at the Fourth Avenue ramp in Point Pleasant on January 13-14.

On Monday, January 8, an ad appears in the *Portsmouth* (Ohio) *Times*. The ad reads in part:

> "*For Lease, approximately 1 acre, 1 mile north of Waverly, Ohio, adjacent to Jerry's Truck Stop, 400 ft. on Route 23. Ideal for gas or oil station. Since the Silver Bridge collapse, all trucks that formerly traveled Route 35, are now using Route 23. Call or write...*"

The ad runs for 4 days.

Simultaneously, the announcement comes that the contract to operate a ferry between Kanauga and Henderson has been granted to Ohio Valley Towing of Glenwillard, Pennsylvania. Operators of the ferry anticipate starting the cross-river service with an 8-car ferry named the "Beaver," running three trips per hour and hauling about 50 cars per hour. The fee will be 50 cents for cars and $2.00-$2.50 for trucks. It is hoped that the service will be up and running by mid-to-late February.

While some of the Civil Defense personnel remain at the

site 24/7 and dragging on the river continues through the week, a large contingent of private boaters join the dragging efforts on the weekend. But no sooner did the weekend effort conclude on Sunday, January 14, than the area is hit with a major snowstorm. Some locations record nearly a foot of snow.

After nearly thirty days, Frank Wamsley is released from Pleasant Valley Hospital. He was admitted the night of the collapse with a broken back. At about the same time, a judge dismisses the case brought by the landowners of the salvage site in Henderson. They have been seeking $8,000 a month and a one-year lease of land now being used to reassemble the bridge.

With several federal and state agencies no longer involved in operations, the recovery shifts to local volunteers. Consequently, John (Andy) Wilson, the head of the Mason County Civil Defense, sends out a plea for volunteers to come and assist with the second round of recovery efforts on January 20–21. Around 54 teams from five states, including Kentucky, Ohio, Tennessee, West Virginia, and Virginia, respond to the appeal. Using a systematic search approach, the crew of each boat is assigned a position and equipped with grabbing hooks, which were fabricated at the Kaiser Aluminum plant in Ravenswood. As operations begin, the volunteers, often as many as five to a boat, are reminded that while 38 bodies have been recovered, eight remain missing. Most impressive, all have agreed to serve without pay. Meals for the volunteers will be served at the Point Pleasant Moose, and all boats will be ordered ashore by 5:00pm. The volunteers will occupy nearly one hundred rooms at the Point Pleasant Resort.

Around 11:30am or so, the Lake County Rescue Team from Painesville, Ohio, recover the body of a young male in his late 20s or early 30s. Using grabbing hooks, the body is recovered about seventy-five feet from the Ohio shore, opposite the mouth of the Kanawha River. The members of the Ohio crew say that the body may have been missed if their boat engine had not gone suddenly dead. The body is the first recovered in nearly three weeks and is immediately taken to

118

the Waugh-Halley-Wood Funeral Home.

Not long after, a second male body, around the same age as the first, is recovered around three-fourths of a mile downstream by a rescue team from Bristol, Tennessee. The body is tagged and transported to the McCoy-Wetherholt Funeral Home in Gallipolis. With the addition of the two bodies, the total number of bodies recovered currently stands at 38.

Just before 9:00am the following morning, a third body is recovered. The body is a male in his late 30s and is found about 500 yards south of the bridge near the Ohio shore. A rescue team from Brookfield (Ohio) Volunteer Fire Department makes the discovery.

In addition to Civil Defense director Wilson announcing a third dragging operation will take place the following weekend, January 27 and 28, the two bodies recovered the day before are identified as Albert Adler and Alonzo "Lonnie" Darst.

As another indication that things continue to wind down around the area, Trinity Methodist Church in Point Pleasant asks individuals who donated food for workers at the disaster site to please come by the church and get their pots or pans. Adding, the church is open daily until 4:00pm.

The horrific news of the capture of the USS Pueblo and its crew of 83 by the North Koreans seems to set the stage for the last eight days of the month. For starters, the third body recovered during the past weekend's dragging operations has been identified as Harold Cundiff of Winston-Salem, North Carolina. Cundiff is reported to have been asleep in the rear of the Hennis Freight Lines truck cab when the bridge fell on December 15. The count of deceased from the bridge collapse now stands at 39, and those still missing number seven.

On Tuesday, January 23, funeral services are held for Alonzo "Lonnie" Darst at the McCoy-Wetherholt Funeral Home, with Rev. John M. Jeffrey officiating. The burial will take place at Gravel Hill Cemetery. He leaves behind a wife and three children, ages 6, 4, and 3. A memorial service for

Albert Adler is scheduled this week in Philadelphia, Pennsylvania. Besides his wife, Adler leaves behind two children, ages 3 years and 18 months

The ferry boat Hustler, owned by the Ohio Valley Ferry Company, arrives in the area, and residents are hoping that ferry service across the river is not far off. With the recovery of a small piece of the wreckage on the Ohio side of the river, federal investigators seem to be honing in on the cause of the bridge's collapse. As a result, the list of possible causes is narrowed to four: wind vibrations, overloading, metal fatigue, and/or design failure. The causes already eliminated include sabotage, breaks in the bridge's deck, and foundation (pier) movements. In the meantime, authorities leading the salvage efforts report that nearly 95% of the bridge elements have been recovered from the water and taken to the salvage site in Henderson.

Deemed as a "last-ditch, all-out last effort" by Mason County Civil Director John (Andy) Wilson, a third-weekend effort at recovering bodies takes place the last weekend of the month. The Saturday search alone includes over 300 volunteers and over sixty small crafts. Searching the waters on the south side of the collapsed bridge, the divers from the U.S. Navy's Explosive Ordnance Demolition Unit discover pockets at least 5 feet deep at the bottom of the riverbed. Unfortunately, the pockets are too deep to use a grabbing hook. Officials feel that the last car to be recovered, a late model Chevrolet belonging to Howard Boggs, may be in one of these pockets.

Sure enough, divers discover a car about 125 feet from the Ohio shore and approximately 30 feet downstream from the Ohio pier. It is car number 24 on the list of vehicles on the bridge at the time of the collapse. As the car is lifted, two bodies are found inside, a young female, possibly in her early 20s, and a young child, around 2 years old. The female is discovered to be holding the child in her arms. Officials immediately contact Howard Boggs, who is assisting in the search but at another location, to identify the bodies. It does not take long for him to be found. Despite being on crutches most of the time, Boggs has only missed one day of dragging since being released from the Pleasant Valley Hospital on December 19th. The bodies inside the car are identified as his wife, Marjorie, and their 17-month-old daughter, Kristy. Their bodies are immediately taken to Waugh-Halley-Wood Funeral Home. Officials believe the Boggs car slid off the twisting bridge like many other vehicles. It was then crushed into the river bottom when tons of steel fell on top. Although the search for additional bodies is called off at dark, the recovery operations are set to resume the next day, beginning at 9:00am.

Some attribute the delay in finding the mother and child to Howard Boggs himself. It is believed that he was giving searchers the wrong location where the car seems to have fallen into the river.

Further, local officials believe that the Boggs car may have been discovered on January 3rd as the Coast Guard began using metal detection devices. It is thought that the members were following up on a report by a man purported to have seen the top of a red car floating near the mouth of Chickamauga Creek on December 16. However, the search team members may have concluded that it was merely steel from the bridge's structure since a great deal of steel remained in the water.

Four landings sites are being considered for the new ferry service that will hopefully begin soon. One of the sites on the east side of the river will be located at Main Street in Point Pleasant, and the other near Henderson. On the Ohio side, a site at Kanauga is being explored. The second site on the west side of the river is yet to be determined. A towboat with the capacity to push a 15-car ferry is en route from Uniontown, Kentucky. An 8-car ferry from Sistersville, West Virginia, is also on its way to the area.

Participating in the January 27-28 dragging operations are over thirty-five units from nearly thirty-five counties around Ohio. While almost 135 persons show up, many boats have 3 or more persons in each boat. Search teams from as far away as Montgomery and Shelby County in western Ohio, Butler County in southeastern Ohio, and Wyandot County near

Sandusky hunt for the five missing bodies. Besides search crews from Charlottesville, Virginia, Harlan County, Kentucky, and Johnson City, Tennessee, teams from Gallia and Meigs Counties, including members of the Gray Ladies and the Red Cross, assist in the weekend campaign.

On Sunday afternoon, January 28, simultaneous memorial services are held on both sides of the river for the victims. One benefit is held in the auditorium of Point Pleasant High School. At the same time, the other takes place at the Gallia Academy High School in Gallipolis. The similar services include Old Testament readings from Isaiah 40:28-31 and Psalm 23. Appropriately, the New Testament readings come from John 14:16 and selected passages from the Letters of the Apostle Paul. As relatives of the victims enter, they are given a red or pink rose.

On Monday, January 29, records are shared with the public surrounding the maintenance and upkeep of the bridge. According to officials, less than $53,000 has been spent on bridge repairs in the last decade. In the fiscal year 1962-63, around $16,000 was spent on roadway lighting and patch work, and less than $1,200 was spent the following year, mostly on lighting the bridge. As for fiscal year 1964-65, nearly $30,000 is spent replacing deteriorating sidewalks, navigation lights, and routine maintenance. During 1966-67, less than $275 is expended on regular maintenance. As for the fiscal year 1967-68, records indicate that nearly $2,400 was spent replacing damaged light standards, widening an approach, installing guardrails, and routine maintenance. Officials report no records are available for the fiscal year 1965-66.

Next to the last day of the month, a joint funeral service is held for Marjorie and Kristy Ann Boggs. The service begins at 2:00pm at Poplar Ridge Church in Vinton, Ohio, with Rev. John Jeffers presiding. The burial is at Mound Hill Cemetery. The bodies of Margaret and Kristy will mark the third body interred at the cemetery from the bridge collapse. Frederick Miller was buried at Mound Hill on December 28.

With the general scope of their work complete, the Corps. of Engineers offers a report on February 5 for the official operations at the collapse site. The report indicates that over 15,000 hours of manpower were spent on diving, heavy equipment operations, rigging, etc. There were no injuries reported. The total cost for the Corps' participation in the search, recovery, and salvage operations is just over $235,000. A breakdown of this amount includes an in-house subtotal of over $46,000 for direct labor, over $6,000 for travel and transportation expenses, and nearly $43,000 for equipment rental and supplies. Outside costs paid to contractors and supplies total over $140,000. Of this amount, the cost to rent the derricks and the personnel to operate them hovers around $71,000. Marine Contracting Services is paid nearly $51,000 for divers, etc. In like manner, the M. T. Epling Company is paid over $16,000 for the use of derrick boats and laborers.

No sooner had the Corps' report been submitted than word comes down from Washington, DC, recognizing Mason County Civil Defense director John (Andy) Wilson's tireless work in the days following the bridge's collapse. Taking special note of Wilson's efforts is Sargent Shriver, the Director of the Office of Economic Development. In writing to West Virginia Governor, Hulett Smith, Shriver points out that Wilson's "...work confirms again the commitment and dedication of the men and women working in the war on poverty" *(Athens Messenger*, February 5, 1968).

On the same day as the opening of the X Olympics Games in Grenoble, France, two area fishermen from Manchester, Ohio, are attempting to salvage a sunken boat. Suddenly, the two men come upon a body caught in the willows of the receding Ohio River. The two men search the body for identification and find a wallet in one of the person's pockets. The body is that of Denzil Taylor. After nearly fifty-five days, his body has ended up around 120 miles south of the Silver Bridge. Taylor's remains will be interred next to his wife's at the IOOF Cemetery, and no funeral is planned.

Although construction on the 60-foot landing site for the ferry in Kanauga is set to begin this week, those on both sides of the Ohio hope full ferry service will start shortly after that. Until then, those who work on the opposite side of the river from where they live will continue to make the 40-50 mile round trip using the Pomeroy Bridge. In the interim, preparations are underway for the fourth weekend of dragging in as many weeks. Six Navy divers are making their way to the bridge collapse site. While two divers are driving trucks loaded with equipment from Charleston, South Carolina, the other four divers are being air lifted to the site from their base in Elizabeth City, North Carolina. The construction has begun on the 60-foot landing site for the ferry in Kanauga.

Near-zero temperatures and choppy waters greet those who volunteer for the fourth weekend of dragging, Feb. 10-11. The search is scheduled to begin at 8:00am each day. Beyond dragging the waters south of the site, the workers, two-thirds from Tennessee, continue to check for debris along the shoreline on both sides of the river. The Ohio Office of Civil Defense will lead the dragging operation in the Gallipolis area. A similar operation will take place on the West Virginia side. Boats launching at Gallipolis will work downstream toward the Gallipolis Locks. Those crews launching in Point Pleasant will work from the site of the bridge collapse downstream toward Gallipolis. Lodging, meals, and fuel for the boats will be provided.

President Johnson labels the collapse a national disaster with economic losses estimated at $1,000,000 a month to the area. Furthermore, the president believes the absence of a bridge constitutes a national emergency. Subsequently, the president orders federal and state governments to begin work on a new bridge to re-connect the two states. In addition to announcing federal monies estimated to be over $6,000,000, President Johnson vows the new bridge will be built in half the time it usually takes a bridge to be constructed. On the day the bidding for the new bridge is introduced in Charleston, a representative from the E. Lionel Pavlo Engineering Company of New York suggests that his company will use the preliminary drawings previously prepared for the I-20 Mississippi River bridge at Vicksburg, Mississippi, to expedite the bridge construction process. The representative adds that the plans will be altered to fit the topography and should be done in the next sixty days or so.

Demonstrating the economic loss, one business in the area reports that monthly gross receipts have dropped from nearly $50,000 to less than $7,000. Of the four truck stops along the Route 35 corridor from Charleston to Columbus before the collapse, one has already closed its doors.

Several sites are being proposed for a new 1,800-foot long, four-lane bridge across the Ohio River that will connect West Virginia with Ohio. One site is in Henderson, with an estimated cost of nearly $13,000,000. The western side of the bridge will be in the city of Gallipolis. A second site is located south of the New York Central railroad trestle and will cost between $11,000,000 and $12,000,000. The third and fourth sites are north of the railroad trestle, and the estimated cost of each is around $12,000,000. In both cases, the eastern entrance to the new bridge is located in Point Pleasant. Whatever site is chosen, the site must first be approved by the Coast Guard since they control navigation on the Ohio River. Subsequently, other suggestions are eliminated, including building a tunnel under the river and constructing an all-aluminum bridge using the old piers as support.

Naturally, there are advantages and disadvantages mentioned for each site. The choice of the first site in Henderson brings a higher cost, as much as $2,000,000, but less disruption to downtown merchants. For obvious reasons, executives from the Goodyear Plant located south of Point Pleasant are pushing for the Henderson site because it will be easier for their workers to get to and from the plant. Some barge and towboat companies favor the Henderson site because their boats will not have to deal with the tricky currents from the confluence of the Kanawha and Ohio Rivers. Conversely, other barge owners believe the proposed location of the bridge's piers at the Henderson location could pose navigational issues for those boats entering or exiting the Kanawha River.

The advantages of the alternate sites include increased traffic flow to the Point Pleasant businesses and a less expensive cost to construct the bridge. Additionally, some believe a location further upstream on the Ohio would better serve any industrial expansion. Among the disadvantages is that some city buildings and homes in Point Pleasant will need to be demolished. There will also be disruption of established traffic patterns downtown, say nothing of the added noise the construction will make for residents and local businesses.

Two ferries, the Beaver and the Hustler, have been docked in Point Pleasant for a month as they await a truck landing site in Henderson and repair to the Main Street landing in Point Pleasant. Several days later, there is good news. At 3:00pm, on Friday, February 23, the Hustler makes the initial ferry run across the river. Except for the Doodlebug train which carried only people, there has not been direct cross-river traffic between Point Pleasant and Kanauga since the bridge collapsed nearly seventy days ago. Sadly, the 15-vehicle Hustler will be the only ferry in service. The 8-car ferry, Beaver, is withdrawn from service after the landing site in Point Pleasant is deemed unsuitable. The boarding site for the larger ferry on the West Virginia side is near Route 17 and Route 2 in Henderson. Rates are 25 cents for foot passengers and 50 cents for cars and small trucks. The rate for larger trucks and buses ranges from $1.50 to $10.00. The ferry service begins the following day, Saturday, February 24. As expected, vehicles are lined up for several blocks because only one ferry is operating. At dusk the next day, a line of no less than forty-five vehicles is lined up on the eastern side of the river, awaiting their turns. It seems that just as many vehicles are waiting on the Ohio side of the river.

A fifth weekend of dragging takes place in an attempt to recover the four bodies still missing from the bridge's collapse. This includes the bodies of Kathy Byus, Thomas Cantrell,

Ronald Sims, and Maxine Turner. Civil Defense directors on both sides of the Ohio, John (Andy) Wilson and John Epling, continue to plead with residents to watch for items along the shoreline. The appeal is timely since the river level has been as much as twelve feet above normal the past several days.

Due to the high volume of vehicles using the ferry and waning interest in train service, local officials announce that the commuter train running between Point Pleasant and Kanauga/Gallipolis will end on February 29.

February ends on a not-so-good note for the boys' basketball team of Point Pleasant High School, coached by Jimmy Joe Wedge. After winning their opening game of the season on Friday, December 15, by one point over Ripley, the team wins only one more game the remainder of the season. They end the regular season with a 2-18 record.

While it may be of little consequence to most drivers in the area, it has been announced that the St. Marys Bridge, located upstream approximately eighty miles, has been reopened after nearly two months. However, because it was constructed using eyebars similar to those used on the Silver Bridge, the St. Marys Bridge was closed three days after the Silver Bridge collapse for safety reasons.

The Corps. of Engineers offer an interim report on the bridge collapse in early March. At the time of the collapse, they report there were 67 people on the bridge in 31 cars. Of that number, nearly one-third escaped injury or were rescued from the water. The total number of fatalities is 46, of which five were immediately killed on the Ohio shore from the collapse. Forty-two bodies have been recovered, and four remain missing. All twenty-four vehicles that dropped from the bridge into the river on December 15, 1967, have been recovered. The last vehicle, a late model Chevrolet, was recovered on January 28. While salvage operations are essentially complete, the remainder of the steel from the bridge's superstructure is expected to be removed entirely by the summer.

On the first weekend of the month, cold temperatures and blowing snow await a group of volunteers who have shown up to search for the remaining four bodies. As volunteers drag the waters of the Ohio, several members of the 24 Key Club of Gallia Academy High School will walk the banks of the western side of the river between the site of the collapse and the Gallipolis Dam.

The bad weather does not keep people from attending the benefit concert of the 85-member Indianapolis Symphony Orchestra on Saturday evening, March 2, at the Gallia Academy High School in Gallipolis. The symphony, on a 21-day tour that will take them as far south as Miami, Florida, will take time from their schedule to help raise funds for the families of the victims of the bridge collapse. Following their stop in the area, the group will head to Bluefield, West Virginia, for a concert Sunday night.

Approximately 100-125 workers from the Goodyear Tire and Rubber Company who live on the Ohio side of the river but work across the Ohio in Apple Grove have started their own ferry service. They meet, park their cars, board a small boat just below the Gallipolis Dam, and travel to the West Virginia shore. Once on the other side, they gather in junk cars and drive to the Goodyear Plant.

However, tragedy strikes on March 14. Just after midnight, four workers who had just finished their shift at the plant begin making their way across the river. Not long after getting into a small boat and heading across the river toward Gallipolis, the motor on the boat suddenly hits a piece of driftwood, and the boat becomes immobilized. The river's swift current carries the boat into a nearby barge, causing the boat to capsize. All four men are thrown into the cold waters of the Ohio. Moreover, they suddenly find themselves under the barge. The men were all wearing lifejackets, and all four quickly surface. However, only two of the men are able to swim back to the West Virginia shore. The other two workers are swept downriver. Their bodies are found just after 9:00am, south of Huntington, near

128

Burlington, Ohio. The river's swift current has carried the bodies of the two men around 35 miles in a matter of hours. This makes four Goodyear employees that have died tragically in the last three months. Albert Adler and Bobby Head were on the Silver Bridge when it collapsed. Their bodies have been recovered. Another Goodyear employee, Ronald Sims, who was riding in the car with Head, remains missing.

Interestingly, it is believed that Silver Bridge survivor and riverboat captain, Howard Boggs, may have been one of the first persons to spot the capsized boat. He had recently returned to work following the death of his wife and daughter.

Speaking of ferry service, it seems the efforts to transport people from one side of the river have hit a bump. Because the ferry landing located at Main Street in Point Pleasant recently caved in, this causes the smaller ferry, the Beaver, to cancel service until repairs are completed. If all goes well, the landing should be back in operation by the end of the month. If the volume of vehicles using the service continues, a second 15-vehicle ferry will join the fleet by mid-May. Should a third multi-vehicle ferry be needed, it will go into service in June. According to the contract with the ferry company, the additional 15-vehicle ferry, towed by the tugboat Sarah, will be ready to go into service in six weeks, pending inspection and approval by the Coast Guard. When the volume of traffic crossing the river begins to exceed service, a second landing may be necessary, one for cars and one for trucks. In that case, cars will be transported from the Main Street landing in Point Pleasant and trucks from the Henderson ramp.

However, it seems the growing pains of the ferry service continue. Not long after departing the landing site in Henderson at the height of rush hour on March 6, the towboat Candy K, called in less than 24 hours before to replace the broken down Hustler towboat, breaks down near the mouth of the Kanawha River. Although the ferry eventually makes it back to shore, it is reported that it may have been helpless in the water for as many as three hours. Adding insult to injury, a pregnant woman aboard the broken down 15-vehicle ferry

129

begins having contractions. When the Candy K arrives back in Henderson, the expectant mother contacts the City Ice and Fuel Company, the same company that was instrumental in saving several people the night of the bridge collapse. Before long, a boat arrives and transports the pregnant woman to the Ohio side of the river, where an ambulance is waiting to take the woman to Holzer Hospital. Less than 12 hours later, the new mother and the new father, currently on a tour of duty in Vietnam, welcome a baby girl. It is believed that residents in the area go two days without ferry service before the backup ferry, the Beaver, arrives to take over ferrying vehicles across the river. As luck would have it, the smaller ferry is in operation less than 24 hours before it develops rudder issues. There is talk that if the ferry service continues to break down, there could be a restart to train commuter service. Thankfully, a new towboat, the Dessie Y, from Owensboro, Kentucky, is in drydock and should be ready for service shortly. This should assist with resolving the vehicle backlog.

Three months to the day after the bridge collapse, Dr. Charles Holzer, Jr., presents a check to the Silver Bridge Disaster fund for nearly $1,300. The money comes from the proceeds of the benefit concert held earlier in the month. The Rev. Gaston Boyle, the pastor at the Point Pleasant Presbyterian Church and head of the relief fund committee, reports that funds in the relief coffer are over $5,000. Some donations have come from as far away as Massachusetts.

On the same day, a reporter from an 11-member team of UPI reporters visits the area for a follow-up article. Before long, the syndicated article appears with a telling story of increasing economic struggle for many in the aftermath of the bridge's collapse. Beyond the increase of nearly $20 for truckers forced to travel to Huntington or Pomeroy to cross the river, the reporter says there have been approximately 100 individuals that have lost their jobs, equaling almost $400,000 in lost income. In particular, the article mentions the financial hardship facing the wife and daughter of James Meadows. When the bridge fell, he died along with his son and mother-in-law, Alma Duff. After subtracting the rent for their apartment, little remains from the monthly $150 benefit check Mrs. Meadows receives from the government.

Due to high water that will create unsafe currents on the river, the planned dragging operations for the third weekend of the month have been called off. It is believed that the water level on the river is approximately 40 feet. However, Civil Defense directors on both sides of the river are seeking volunteers to participate in recovery efforts the following weekend, March 23 and 24. The Coast Guard reports there is no longer any steel on the bottom of the river that is large enough to cover a vehicle or a body.

At the American Legion of Point Pleasant monthly meeting on March 16, Mason County Civil Defense director John (Andy) Wilson is presented the Legion Medal of Merit for his tireless efforts surrounding the bridge disaster on December 15. This is only the second time in the post's history that such an award is presented. The first time was nearly 5-years ago when a newspaper boy was delivering papers and reported a fire at the Episcopal Church on Main Street in Point Pleasant.

Under the leadership of West Virginia Senator Jennings Randolph, Chairman of the Senate Committee on Public Works, hearings continue on ways to prevent another bridge collapse. On March 18, the committee hears testimony from a federal official who declares that the Point Pleasant bridge is not the federal government's responsibility. The official adds that the bridge was not built with federal aid; therefore, it does not need to be inspected by federal inspectors.

Of the three groups appointed by the NTSB to work on the collapse, the bridge design group continues looking into the bridge's history from when it was built in 1928 to the present. The last of the three groups, the structural analysis and tests group under the direction of Charles Scheffey, continue looking into the components used to construct the bridge.

On the last Friday of the month, the all-sports banquet is held at Point Pleasant High School, and the first annual "Golden Shoe" is awarded. The award, presented by the Rardin

Shoe Center, is in memory of the school's former teacher and coach, James White. The school's boys' head basketball coach, Jimmy Joe Wedge, son of bridge victims Paul and Lillian Wedge, presents awards at the banquet to his players.

Near the time the world receives the tragic news of the assassination of Dr. Martin Luther King, Jr., in Memphis, Tennessee, residents on both sides of the river receive word that ferry service is back in full operation. Naturally, the ferry's capacity to carry multiple cars meets with applause from residents on both shorelines. Residents report seeing the ferry crisscrossing the river every 10-minutes or so. This comes as good news in light of the company's recent mechanical failures. Still, not all is well.

On the West Virginia side of the river, a grievance has been filed with the city of Point Pleasant regarding the quality of ferry service. The complaint states that the ferry company has failed to meet the contract terms. Specifically, the petition cites that the landing points are inadequate and unsafe. In addition, schedules are not being met, and wait time for service across the river can sometimes be as long as 2-3 hours. Finally, the petition states that the service cannot currently handle the volume of traffic. If the Ohio Valley Towing Company cannot keep to the terms of the contract, the petition demands that they be let go. In the meantime, it is being reported that another ferry service is interested in the contract. The mechanical problems of the company's towboats are in addition to the other issues created by mother nature, like fog and rough water on the river. Needless to say, by the second full week of April, a 15-vehicle ferry and the smaller, 8-vehicle ferry are in service and running at full capacity.

As riots continue in countless U.S. cities following Dr. King's assassination, a dredge from the Corps. of Engineers is returning to the site of the bridge collapse after nearly four months. Hopefully, the weekend effort will find the missing eyebar pin from Section 330 of the bridge's suspension chain.

132

This is the first attempt by the Corps. to locate the missing pin, which is 18-inches in length, 12-inches wide, and weighs about 300 pounds. Those tasked with reassembling the bridge at the site in Henderson believe the missing pin may offer additional insight into the bridge's collapse. The search for the missing pin is scheduled to begin shortly after sunrise on Friday, April 12, and again the following day at the same time if the pin is not located. Dredging for the weekend will conclude at 11:00pm on Saturday, April 13th. There will be no dredging on Easter Sunday, April 14th. It is believed that during one of the dredging days by the Corps. that the missing part of the fractured eyebar (N330) is retrieved.

As the last full week of April begins, Point Pleasant High School announces that a Silver Bridge Memorial Book Fund has been established. The idea originates with the members of the school's Library Service Club. Moreover, the club members vote to spend a portion of their earned money to purchase books for the school library. A second club at the school, the Interact Club, quickly responds to the book challenge by giving $60 toward the purchase of a 10-volume set of *The International Library of Negro Life and History*. Before long, several other clubs in the school agree to participate in the effort, including the Key Club, the FTC (Future Teachers Club), and the FBL (Future Business Leaders). Going forward, all books purchased as part of the fund-raiser will have an inscription inside the book that reads in part "In Memory of the Victims of the Bridge Disaster 1967."

On the last weekend of the month, the Coast Guard Depot at Point Pleasant receives word from a tugboat that a body has been spotted on the river north of Huntington. The Coast Guard reports searching the area for nearly two hours but fails to locate a body.

At the same time, news comes that the new bridge's site will be about one-quarter mile south of Henderson. The approach to the new bridge on the West Virginia side will be just south of the Henderson School. The Ohio landing will be located near Baird Wrecking Service. A cloverleaf exchange will connect the bridge to Route 35 and Route 7. To further speed up construction, it is announced that the superstructure components will be fabricated offsite while the piers are being constructed. Additionally, the new bridge design contract has been awarded to the Pavlo firm.

Around the time that U.S. negotiator W. Averell Harriman, and the chief negotiator for the North Vietnamese, Xuan Huy, are meeting in Paris for preliminary peace talks to end the war in Vietnam, the NTSB begins a series of hearings in Charleston surrounding the collapse of the Silver Bridge.

During the second day of hearings on May 8th, it seems that a faulty traffic light at the western end of the bridge that dumps traffic onto Route 7 in Ohio has become a hot topic. One of the thirty-three witnesses called to testify is Paul Scott, who survived the collapse. Scott testifies that he and his two friends in the car, James Pullen and Frederick Miller, were on the bridge long enough that they had "four full bull sessions." Pullen and Miller die in the collapse, and their bodies are recovered the day after Christmas. Another person, Floyd Forbus, testifies that he saw a large nut lying on the roadway when he crossed the bridge earlier in the day on December 15. A third witness to testify during the hearings is Wesley Wears, an employee with the City Fuel and Ice Company. As part of a rescue team that saved several lives the night of the collapse, Wears testifies that the middle span of the bridge broke in the middle, and vehicles fell straight down, almost as if they were falling into a funnel. Some of the vehicles, he tells the court of inquiry, fell backward while others fell forward. Wears adds that some of the vehicles fell off the bridge rather than with it, and that vehicles had a short drop and then a fatal one into the river.

At the same hearings, a veteran bridge inspector testifies that the last complete bridge inspection he performed took place in 1951 and was conducted mainly with binoculars. Additionally, when pressed further on the issue, he confesses that he followed less than half of the required procedures when he inspected the Silver Bridge in 1965. The inspector adds that the inspection was made with an eye toward maintenance and repairs. However, he did not have binoculars at the 1965 inspection. As for the reported inspections in 1963 and 1964, it seems they were done with binoculars. On nearly a dozen inspection items, including an inspection of the top of the towers, the inspector reports not using the company manual as a guide.

During the 4th and last day of testimony on May 10, it is disclosed for the first time that bridge investigators discovered a crack in one of the hanger connectors that run vertically from the eyebars chains to the deck. The investigator offering the testimony says the crack is found while examining parts of the bridge at the salvage site. Still, investigators are convinced that if they can find the missing pin for section C-330, the pin that connected the cracked eyebar to an adjacent eyebar, a great deal could be answered. The pin may hold the cause of the collapse. To date, the pin remains missing.

Meanwhile, the word also reaches residents on both sides of the river that investigators have made some conclusions regarding possible causes of the collapse. The items already ruled out include sabotage, breaks in the bridge's deck, and weakening of the piers caused by previous barge accidents. Additional causes no longer considered are displacement of anchorages, wind, and overload of vehicles.

Not only has the work on the Ohio approach begun with the dumping of several tons of fill dirt, but it is being reported that the core drilling for the bridge's piers has been completed. Approaches on the West Virginia side are located just north of the site where the old bridge is being reassembled. Despite the good news regarding progress about the new bridge, two private homes, and one business, the Dance Service Station, all located in the new bridge area on the Ohio side of the river, have been condemned. One resident has been in her home for over two decades and is given less than a week to vacate.

On the Friday before Mother's Day, a lawsuit is filed in Kanawha Circuit Court in Charleston, West Virginia, by Mary Ethel Rouse, administrator of the estate of Leo Blackman. The plaintiff is asking for $1,000,000 in damages and an additional $1,000,000 for punitive and exemplary damages. The defendants named in the suit are the J. E. Greiner Company, who designed the plans for the Silver Bridge, and U.S. Steel, who provided the steel. A subsidiary of U.S. Steel, American Bridge Corporation, built the superstructure. The complaint alleges the defendants are negligent in the design, supplying a defective piece of material, and/or construction of the bridge.

On the same day, four additional suits are filed by Clara Towe, administrator of the estate of Robert Towe, Nancy Bennett for Julius Bennett, Marie Cundiff for Harold Cundiff, and Judy Mabe for Gene Mabe. As with the Blackman filing, the plaintiffs cite the same defendants. Beyond claiming negligence on the part of the defendants, the last four filings claim the plaintiffs have funeral expenses over $1,500 and the administrators of the estate have sustained financial damages. According to West Virginia law and previous court decisions, lawyers for the defendants argue that no compensation can be paid if the cause is not pinpointed. Further, lawyers for the defendants say the bridge's collapse is an act of God. It will be up to the plaintiffs to prove negligence and that the defendants knew about the cause and did nothing. According to Ohio law, the state of Ohio is immune.

Moreover, all five plaintiffs in the lawsuit are long-haul truckers who lived outside the immediate area of the bridge collapse. Julius Bennett and Gene Mabe are from North Carolina and were employed by Roadway Express. Towe, a resident of Virginia, was also employed by Roadway Express. Cundiff, a driver for Hennis Freight Lines, is also from North Carolina. The last of the five plaintiffs, Leo Blackman, also from Virginia, was a driver for Transcon at the time of his death.

Just before 3:00pm on Mother's Day, two men in a private

boat are cruising on the Ohio River when they spot a body in the water some three miles south of Gallipolis, near Clipper Mills. The two men pull the body as close to the Ohio shore as possible. As one of the men stays with the body, the second man jumps in the river and swims toward the shore. No sooner has the second man reached shore than he contacts Gallia County Sheriff Denver Walker to report the discovery. Before long, the body is identified as that of Thomas Cantrell. Cantrell's body, the 43rd to be recovered, has been missing for nearly 150 days. This leaves three bodies still missing: Kathy Byus, Ronald Sims, and Maxine Turner. The funeral service for Cantrell is set for Tuesday, May 14, at the First Baptist Church, beginning at 2:00pm. Officiating is Rev. Joseph Chapman, and the interment will be at Mound Hill Cemetery.

The same week the Ohio River again tops the 40-foot level, the Point Pleasant Resort reopens as the Pleasant Point Resort. Meanwhile, sealed bids are being opened to construct the Route 35 overpass in Gallipolis. The new overpass will be approximately 200 feet in length.

At the Point Pleasant High School Awards Day ceremony, the first annual Paul and Lillian Wedge Scholarship is given out.

———————

No sooner had my oldest brother, Frank, begun his 15-month deployment in Bac Lieu, South Vietnam, than the sealed bids are being opened in Charleston, West Virginia, for the different phases of construction for the new bridge. The first contract is awarded to Allied Structural Steel Company of Hammond, Indiana. They will build the Ohio abutment and one pier for just over $124,000 and construct the bridge's superstructure for just over $5,000,000. The Al Johnson Construction Company of Minneapolis, Minnesota, agrees to build piers two and three for $1,300,000. The sections of the superstructure will be fabricated at Knoxville, Tennessee, Plainfield, New Jersey, and Hammond. The fabricated parts will then be transported by rail to the new bridge site to be assembled. While the current cost of the bridge without approaches is estimated to be nearly $11,000,000, the price will be shared by the federal government and the states at both ends of the bridge. The design firm of Howard, Needles, Tammen, and Bergendorf is awarded the contract to design the four new piers and two abutments for the bridge. With a bid of nearly $2,100,000, the S. J. Groves and Sons Company of Minneapolis, Minnesota, is awarded the contract to construct the approach on the eastern side of the Ohio. The remaining contract will be awarded for the bridge's deck and lighting.

As Henderson residents complain of excessive dust at the ferry landing, it is decided to black-top the road leading to the ferry. The work will be done by the Black Rock Company of Charleston. Even though the Point Pleasant landing at Main Street has not been used for some time, it will also be black-topped. When the new 15-vehicle ferry is ready for use, the 8-vehicle ferry will resume service at the Point Pleasant landing.

As two men from Huntington are fishing nine miles or so south of the collapse site on Saturday, June 22, they spot a body caught on a fallen tree on the Ohio side of the river. Immediately, the men notify local authorities. The body is later identified as Ronald Sims. It is the 44th person to be recovered from the bridge collapse. Sims' body, missing for nearly one hundred and sixty days, is found not far from the Goodyear Plant where he worked. He is the third Goodyear employee on the bridge the evening of the collapse to die. The body of Albert Adler was recovered on January 27. The body of Robert Head, the driver of the car in which Sims was a passenger, was recovered on Christmas Eve.

A memorial service for Ronald Sims is set for Wednesday, June 26, in Weston, West Virginia, with L. Curtis Saville officiating. Following Masonic rites, the body will be interred at the Masonic Cemetery of Weston. Sims leaves behind a wife and three young children, a boy, age 9, and younger twin girls. Although there was a memorial service held earlier in the month for Sims, his body remained missing. The delay in finding his body caused significant family hardship. Not only did it prevent them from gaining a sense of closure, but without a death certificate, the family was not eligible for many critical services.

As the second half of the year begins, the first signs on the western side of the new bridge begin to appear. The builders report that the concrete for the Ohio approach has been poured and is near completion. Before the week is out, the cranes from the Al Johnson Company, the company contracted to build piers two and three, arrive in Point Pleasant.

Sadly, news has been received of the first death of a person to die who had a relative pass away from the collapse. Frederick Taylor, the father of Denzil Taylor, passes away on July 9, exactly five months to the day that his son was laid to rest. Frederick Taylor is not only buried in the same cemetery where his son and daughter-in-law, Glenna, are buried, the International Order of Odd Fellows Cemetery in Harrisville, West Virginia but in the same family plot. The elder Taylor was in his early 50s.

Those looking for a picture of the Silver Bridge for sentimental reasons are told to be aware. It seems a great many postcards are being sold, especially in West Virginia state parks, that display a bridge on the front of the card and a description of the Silver Bridge on the back. The only problem is that the picture on the front of the postcard is not the Silver Bridge. While the description on the back of the card is that of the old bridge, the picture on the front of the postcard is actually the Shadle Bridge over the Kanawha River, south of Point Pleasant.

On the next to the last day of the month, the first accident occurs during the construction of the new bridge. Reports are that a crane topples over due to overloading. The accident does not involve a death or a worker with injuries.

The state of West Virginia has been told that it will be receiving nearly $147,000,000 in funds as part of the Federal-

Aid Highway Act. The state will put around $7,000,000 of that toward its part of the construction costs for the new bridge.

As movie goers anticipate the arrival of *The Green Berets* starring John Wayne to the State Theater in downtown Point Pleasant, residents on both sides of the Ohio become aware of a story in the August 4 edition of the *Cleveland Plain Dealer Sunday Magazine*. The multi-page article is a follow-up story written by the same reporter who penned the article on Melvin Cantrell's funeral several months earlier. Residents on both sides of the river are quick to point out the numerous inaccuracies in the article. For starters, the bridge collapsed around 5:00pm on December 15, and not at 6:05pm on December 14, as the article states. In addition, the writer goes on to communicate that the bridge killed people that had little to live for, owned very little, and that ambulance drivers were bored waiting for bodies to be recovered. However, the writer was most critical of the Cantrell family and their current situation.

Accompanied by a newspaper photographer, the writer shares that during his 60-90 minute interview with the Cantrell family, many of the children are wearing dirty clothes. Additionally, most were sniffling because the room was cold and the family was out of coal. When the reporter directs his questions at one of the older children, he is told that the family is on ADC (Aid to Dependent Children), not to sit on the sofa because the springs are coming through the cushions, and not to take his shoes off because the floor is dirty. As before, these statements, and countless others, are inaccurate. The family is not on federal or state aid of any form. More, this last interview takes place in August, so how cold could the room be. Finally, all funeral expenses have been paid, and there were around 100 people at the funeral and not 30 or so, as the article states.

As for Mrs. Cantrell, the writer says that she does not speak during the interview. She merely sits there and allows one of her older children to do the talking. Moreover, the writer concludes that Mrs. Cantrell has the same expression she had at her husband's funeral. Furthermore, she will neither talk about what happened nor how the family is doing. Beyond pictures of the underage children without their parent's permission, it is revealed later that Mrs. Cantrell was not at home when the interview takes place.

At the same time, residents on the east side of the Ohio anticipate the opening of the Mason County Fair. The seventh annual fair begins with a kick-off parade on August 6, beginning at 2:00pm. This year, an added attraction will be an 8-foot long and 3-foot high replica of the Silver Bridge. Roy Acuff and his Smoky Mountain Boys will perform on the last night of the fair on Saturday, August 10. This year's Gallia County Fair theme is "Take Me Out to the Fair."

Meanwhile, the Sunshine Sunday School Class at the First Presbyterian Church in Point Pleasant is the first group to contribute to a Memorial Chapel Fund at Pleasant Valley Hospital. When completed, the chapel will be dedicated to those that lost their lives in the collapse. Additionally, the volume of vehicles using the cross-river ferry continues to grow. In fact, another 15-vehicle ferry is scheduled to go into service before the end of the month. This comes as good news since the 8-vehicle ferry is once more out of commission.

In bridge-related news, the construction of the (bridge) piers continues on the West Virginia side with the installation of pilings. Limestone boulders from a quarry in Moundsville, West Virginia, will be laid to support the land pilings and pier.

The hearings convened following the bridge's collapse by West Virginia Senator Jennings Randolph, Chairman of the Senate Committee on Public Works, seem to have paid dividends with the first federal bridge inspection program being incorporated into the Federal-Aid Highway bill. The bill, signed into law by President Johnson on August 24, requires the Department of Transportation to conduct safety inspections for all federally-funded bridges every two years. A National Bridge Inventory is also created to provide a central database where all inspection information and safety ratings could be stored and reviewed.

Around the same time Saundra Williams of Pennsylvania is crowned as the first Miss Black America, the 1967-68 yearbook of Point Pleasant High School arrives for distribution. This year's OH-KAN includes pictures of Denzil and Glenna Taylor and James White, former teachers at the school who passed away when the bridge fell. In addition, the yearbook mentions Paul Wedge, former president of the Mason County Board of Education, and his wife, Lillian.

As the first week of the month ends, it is reported that Paul Scott, a passenger in a car that fell from the Silver Bridge, has filed suit against J. E. Greiner and U.S. Steel. The lawsuit, filed in Kanawha Circuit Court, claims property loss, loss of earning, and permanent injury. Mr. Scott seeks $250,000 in compensatory damages and $1,000,000 in punitive damages. Scott was the lone survivor in the car that killed his co-workers James Pullen and Frederick Miller the night of the bridge collapse.

Along with the bad news that the second cross-river ferry is out of commission, a ferry operated by the Crane Company, there is the good news that the new Gallia-Meigs regional Airport has been dedicated and is ready for business. The airport's 4,000-foot runway is north of Gallipolis and adjacent to the Route 35 by-pass. It is near where the new bridge is being constructed.

As the month comes to a close, a Penn Central train pulling nearly 100 cars of coal becomes stalled on the trestle immediately north of the old bridge. The train began with three engines, but not long after reaching the bridge, the wheels on the third engine begin to drag, causing the engine to smoke. The train, headed for Toledo, Ohio, and Lake Erie, could not pull the load without the third engine. After many of the cars are unhooked, the first train continues on its way with over sixty cars. A second train is called to take the remaining coal cars to their destination.

On the last day of the month, the Ohio Department of Highways announces they are seeking bids to construct the Ohio entrance ramp onto the new bridge. The cost for the approach is estimated to be between $2,000,000 and $3,000,000. The adjusted cost for the new bridge is now being estimated at nearly $12,000,000, with $7,500,000 for the superstructure and $2,500,000 for the West Virginia approach.

As Hurricane Gladys approaches the west coast of Florida and the St. Petersburg/Clearwater area, a $550,000 libel/damage suit is being filed in U.S. District Court in Columbus, Ohio. While the state of West Virginia is not named in the suit, the defendants include the federal government, U.S. Steel, J. E. Greiner Company, the state of Ohio, and the American Bridge Company, a subsidiary of U.S. Steel and the builder of the bridge's superstructure. The plaintiffs in the suit are the children of the deceased, Melvin Cantrell, and the administrator of his estate, his wife, Margaret.

The National Transportation Safety Board issues a 10-month interim report on the bridge collapse. The Board concludes there were 37 vehicles on the bridge at the time of the collapse, 31 fell with the bridge, and 24 fell into the water and were later recovered. Another seven fell with the bridge on the Ohio shore, and six vehicles remained on the bridge. There were no pedestrians on the bridge at the time. Besides a cloudy sky and a light wind from the west, the temperature was 30 degrees. Of the issues initially thought to have caused the bridge's collapse, the Board has ruled out several issues, including sabotage, displacement of anchorage, wind, lack of bridge symmetry (cars on one side of the bridge and pedestrian walkway on the other side), sonic boom, breakage of the eyebar chain in the middle or West Virginia span, the collision of barges on piers, vehicle accident on the bridge before the collapse, and overloading. The issues still being considered focus on metal fatigue, corrosion, and manufacturing defects. At this point, the cause of the failure seems to be pointing toward an issue with the bridge's suspension system.

One month after the August 8th article appears in print, Margaret Cantrell and her seven children (Lolita, Dora, William, Juanita, Terry, Nancy, and Keith) bring suit against the *Cleveland Plain Dealer* and three other defendants, including the newspaper's publishing company, Forest City Publishing, the article's writer, and the photographer. The suit claims that the 5-page story, along with the photographs, contains gross errors and misrepresentations that the Cantrell family are hillbillies, unclean, and backward. The plaintiffs are seeking $1,000,000 in damages.

The final football game of the year between the Black Bears of Point Pleasant High School and Gallia Academy High School will be different this time. Usually, the visiting team will take the short drive across the Ohio River, but not this year. This year, the visitors must travel north around 20 miles to the Pomeroy Bridge, traverse the bridge, and then travel another 20 miles south to their opponent's field. In prior years, the same round trip would take less than 30-minutes. It will now take upwards of 60-90 minutes for the team to travel.

As proceedings to condemn land for public use for the West Virginia approach to the bridge are moved from Mason County Circuit Court to Kanawha County Circuit Court, the chairman of the federal panel investigating the bridge collapse tells state legislators that no one could have foreseen the disaster. Moreover, the chairman adds that no one could have assessed the bridge's condition without dismantling it and testing the parts. Subsequently, the official states that poor inspection can be ruled out as a cause of the collapse. The official reiterates the belief that the eyebar nearest the Ohio tower lay at the center of the collapse. However, upcoming tests on materials will tell the truth. At the same meetings, another official seems to challenge the chairman's statement by saying that the cause of the collapse is metal fatigue.

As workers continue to put in 10-hour days, 6 days a week, to get the new bridge built by the proposed completion date, September 1969, the work on the Ohio approach is nearly complete. As for the other side of the river, the shore piers were finished earlier in the month, and work on the two river piers is underway. To the north of the new bridge construction site, the fourth search in as many weeks is taking place for the missing pin that connected the two eyebars in question. Finding the missing pin is crucial because it could tell if the pin came out first, and then the eyebar gave way, or did the eyebar fracture, and then the pin came out. The three previous attempts by the Corps. of Engineers to find the missing pin has cost nearly $30,000.

On Wednesday, November 20, the state of West Virginia is hit with a second tragedy in less than a year. To those that remember, the disaster is referenced in three words: "Farmington No. 9." On that day, an explosion at a coal mine near Farmington, West Virginia, traps nearly 100 men. Although over twenty of the miners are safely rescued, all efforts at saving the seventy-eight remaining miners are unsuccessful. Days later, the mine is sealed with seventy-eight men inside.

With only a few days remaining until Thanksgiving, sealed bids are opened on the final phase of the new bridge construction. The contract is awarded to Melbourne Brothers Construction Company of North Canton, Ohio. For nearly $650,000, the company will place the span deck and install the lighting. The company will have 120 days to complete the work.To allow ample time for any touch-ups before the final inspection, the dedication date for the new bridge has been moved back to December 15 of next year. The date makes the dedication precisely two years to the day of the collapse of the Silver Bridge. Best of all, there is news that the Federal Highway Act of 1968, signed earlier in the year by President

Johnson, now includes the new bridge being fully funded by the federal government. It was initially announced that West Virginia and Ohio would have to chip in nearly $5,000,000 combined as their contribution toward the construction of the new bridge. Still, the news is tempered by the report that the new bridge may cost as much as $16,000,000, the same amount it cost to construct the Brooklyn Bridge. However, it took thirteen years to complete that bridge, while it is hoped that the new bridge will be completed in two years or less.

With the anniversary of the bridge's collapse only a few weeks away, there is talk on the eastern side of the river that the West Virginia approach to the old bridge will soon be demolished. Sure enough, it isn't long before the West Virginia State Road Commission notifies those on both sides of the river that not only will the West Virginia approach be demolished but the Ohio approach as well. The remaining river piers will also be torn down. The Point Pleasant City Council votes to give the land to the city. One proposal for the use of the site is a park.

The remaining 17 days of the month bring their own share of joys and sorrows. On December 13, an issue develops during the construction of the new pier on the Ohio side. After drilling nearly halfway into the river bottom, the cofferdam protecting the pier pilings springs a leak, causing the dam to fill with water. Divers are sent in to explore and repair. The leak will cause the pouring of the concrete for the piers to be delayed anywhere from 1-3 months. However, workers around the site say they are willing to continue working 24 hours a day to meet the completion deadline. Adding to the woes of some residents, it is announced that the Hi Carpenter Bridge, located nearly 80 miles upstream in St. Marys, will be closed permanently. Inspectors from the NTSB have discovered cracks in some of the internal eyebars. The closing of the Hi Carpenter Bridge and the collapse of the Silver Bridge now means there are only two bridges remaining between New Martinsville and Huntington to transport persons across the Ohio River...the bridge at Pomeroy, and the bridge at Parkersburg. In an action that surprises many, longtime Mason County Civil Defense Director John (Andy) Wilson submits his resignation. Richard Newell, Jr., will take over for Wilson, who has been in the post for six years.

On Tuesday evening, December 17, the Point Pleasant High School boys basketball team snaps a nearly year-long losing streak by beating Parkersburg Catholic by one point. The last time the team won a regular-season game was nearly a year ago.

The Year 1969

A few days before Sirhan Sirhan is scheduled to go on trial for the killing of Sen. Robert Kennedy in Los Angeles, California, the city of Point Pleasant is hit with yet another challenge. Just before 12:00noon on January 3rd, a fire in the downtown area destroys two businesses and damages two others. The fire is believed to have started in the bedroom of a second-floor apartment above the City Pharmacy on Main Street. Aided by whipping winds, the fire quickly spread to the adjacent building, which houses the Music Box. At one point, local authorities feared the fire would consume an entire block. Also suffering extensive smoke and water damage during the fire are Cohen Drug Store, the Ben Franklin Store, and the French City Lumber Company. All are located on the same side of the street as the City Pharmacy. Four fire departments assist the Point Pleasant Fire Department in fighting the fire, including the Ripley Fire Department, the Mason Fire Department, the General Services Administration Depot members, and the Gallipolis Fire Department. The latter group brings their 75-foot ladder-pumper truck across the Ohio River via the ferry. The fire is brought under control by mid-afternoon, and the estimated damages are around $500,000. Once the fire is extinguished, and individuals are allowed to enter the buildings, volunteers can be seen salvaging merchandise and records from the damaged stores. Ironically, this was the manager of the Music Box's first day on the job. Although the downtown area is extensively damaged, the city does not qualify for federal disaster funds.

On the first Tuesday of the month, the $550,000 lawsuit filed in October of last year by Margaret Cantrell and her children on behalf of her deceased husband, Melvin, against the federal government is dismissed. In addition to U.S. Steel denying all charges, they are asking the U.S. District Court in Columbus, Ohio, to dismiss the case against them. The Greiner Company, also a defendant in the lawsuit, is petitioning the court to do the same for them.

Near the last full week of the month, an awards ceremony is held at the Coast Guard Depot and Locks 11 for those who assisted in the search and recovery operations following the bridge collapse. Coast Guard medals are awarded to LTJG J. E. Mason and CWO-2 William E. Jones. Both men spent over two months at the collapse site assisting with operations. Letters of Appreciation were also given to Earl Hysell, William J. McCormick, Larry W. McDaniels, Harley Hartley, and Wesley Wears. The men were part of the City Ice and Fuel boat that rescued survivors dumped into the river's chilly waters the night of the collapse.

No sooner do workers return to the bridge on Thursday morning, February 6, than work is halted due to a jurisdictional labor dispute. A picket line is set up after Laborers Union 543 of Huntington walks off the job. The local claims that its men should have had the job of drilling holes to drive piling for the new bridge piers, not members of the Piledrivers Union. Despite pleas from union representatives and mediators for the men to return to work, the workers refuse. One week later, the strike remains in place. It is believed that the dispute was brought on by a design change for the new bridge.

As the last full week of the month begins, several residents on the east side of the river are told some bad news. The cloverleaf of the new bridge construction on the West Virginia side of the bridge may require demolishing no less than fifteen structures. If the site of the cloverleaf is approved, owners of the structures will have until September to vacate. Standing in the path are the Henderson School and Leona's Diner.

On February 26, a report from the Logan (West Virginia) Civil Defense team states that during search and recovery operations last year, the group spent over 260 hours and six weeks at the site of the bridge's collapse, lending assistance.

With the welcome arrival of spring a few days earlier and daily temperatures in the area nearing the upper 50s, workers begin making arrangements to pour concrete for the bridge piers. According to plans drawn up by the Al Johnson Company, the pouring will start with the West Virginia pier.

With Easter only a few days away, bridge leaders report that work is progressing nicely. The Ohio footers for the two piers on the west side of the river have been poured, and the 75-foot approach to the new bridge is complete. Bridge leaders also state that the West Virginia pier should be completed by next month and the Ohio pier by early June. In addition, a moderate winter with little snowfall reduces the chances of spring flooding. In turn, it is believed that the Ohio River rose only a matter of inches as the piers were being built. This also helps speed the construction of the new bridge along.

Following a thorough inspection by the bridge consulting firm of Modjeski and Masters, the firm recommends that the nearly 65-year-old bridge at Chester/Newell-East Liverpool be closed permanently. Originally built as a suspension bridge in the early 1900s, the bridge is one of the last suspension bridges over the Ohio River. Acting on the recommendation, the bridge is closed immediately. If one includes the Silver Bridge and Hi Carpenter Bridge near St. Marys, this makes the third of ten bridges connecting West Virginia and Ohio now closed.

The day after Mother's Day, a lawsuit is filed in the Circuit Clerk's Office in Point Pleasant by Allied Structural Steel Company. Defendants in the suit are the City of Henderson and the city mayor. Allied Steel, awarded the contract to build one of the piers and construct the superstructure, claims they are being levied an improper business tax on a mobile trailer the company is using as a temporary field office while the bridge is being constructed. Although the bridge is being built outside of city limits, the trailer's location is considered within the city limits of Henderson. Subsequently, the city believes it has a right to levy a tax on the trailer. However, this incident is not the only issue surrounding the new construction.

A few days after Memorial Day, a motorist reports that an object strikes his car as he was traveling under the overpass near the construction site of the new bridge in Gallipolis. The motorist says that an unidentified object did heavy damage to his windshield as he passed the site around 12:00noon. A few hours later, there is an accident involving a truck and a school bus. It seems the truck driver hit the right side of the bus as the driver was attempting to turn onto a dirt road at the construction site. The bus was in the process of passing the truck.

Point Pleasant High School student leaders report that their fund-raising efforts toward purchasing books for the school library are moderately successful. Total donations have reached a point where the school can buy nearly three dozen books for the library.

The pre-fabricated parts for the new bridge's superstructure have begun arriving in the area. As pieces arrive, they will be assembled on-site to expedite the completion of the bridge.

To date, there have been nine lawsuits totaling over $18,000,000 filed in Kanawha County Courts surrounding the loss of lives, injuries, and damages from the Silver Bridge collapse. The biggest of the suits, $6,000,000, is filed by George Byus, who lost a wife and two daughters in the disaster. Filing $2,000,000 suits each were administrators of the estates of Victor Turner, James White, and James Meadows. Those parties seeking $1,250,000 are administrators for the estates of Samuel Frank Ellis and injured parties Frank Wamsley, Paul Hayman, William Edmondson, and Frank Nunn.

With only months remaining until its contract ends, Ohio Valley Towing has applied to the West Virginia Public Service Commission for a rate increase. Owners are asking for a rate increase from 50 to 75 cents for cars and $2.00 to $3.00 per trip for specific trucks. Ferry service across the Ohio began some sixteen months prior.

———————————

Around the time Neil Armstrong sets foot on the moon, American Legion Post 23 of Point Pleasant and Allied Structural Steel Company devise a way to honor the past and mark its future. The two groups are planning to place a beam that will be used to construct the new bridge on display at the ramp of the old bridge on the West Virginia side of the river. For upwards of one week, the public will be invited to write names and sentiments on the beam before the piece is installed on the new bridge. There will be plenty of space for names because the particular piece weighs more than 25 tons and is nearly 90 feet long. The signed beam will be the final section of the top chord of the bridge, and it will be called the Byus-Turner piece in memory of the two bodies not recovered, Kathy Byus and Maxine Turner.

———————————

The bridge work is really beginning to take shape. Since the first of the pre-fabricated steel began arriving in mid-June, workers have been working at an accelerated pace to install the steel as they get the bridge ready for the last major phase of the construction…the decking. The decking is scheduled to begin the153ollowingg month.

By August 10, the West Virginia approach had not only been completed but dedicated in a public ceremony. The ceremony, attended by residents from both sides of the river, seeks to keep alive the memory of those killed in the collapse and remind those in attendance of the bridge's symbolic nature in maintaining the close relationship between the two communities on opposite sides of the river. Frank Wamsley, one of the survivors rescued from the river the night of the collapse and who spent several weeks in the hospital due to his injuries, is present at the ceremony. One of the last acts during the ceremony was the emotional dedication of the Byus-Turner piece, which contains the names of countless residents.

Between June 16 and the second week of August, it is believed that over 7,500 tons of steel have been installed on the superstructure. Designers of the bridge estimated that the installation of the steel would take nearly one hundred days. It has taken less than 60! The last piece of steel, the Byus-Turner piece, was placed just before 2:00pm on August 8. This act figuratively rejoins the two communities. Later the same night, the supervisor of construction of the new bridge hosts a celebratory dinner for nearly one hundred company workers, state road employees, and their guests. The event is held at the Moose Lodge in Point Pleasant.

On August 10, the list of obituaries in the local newspapers included the name of Sadie Meadows of Point Pleasant. She is preceded in death by her son, James Meadows, and her grandson, Timothy Meadows, who passed away in the Silver Bridge collapse. Mrs. Meadows is believed to be the second person to die that had a relative pass away in the collapse. She was 79.

With the season officially over, awards are presented at the Point Pleasant Girls' Softball League ceremony on Tuesday, August 12. Among the awards presented is the Kathy Byus Memorial Plaque for Sportsmanship. Byus played in the league before her untimely passing twenty months ago.

As countless individuals across the U.S. are making their way to Max Yasgur's dairy farm in upstate New York for three days of peace and music (Woodstock), three painters are citing safety concerns about the new bridge. In addition to saying that other painters are simply painting over rust spots on the bridge rather than removing them, the three say there are countless loose bolts among the bridge's 120,000 bolts. When their supervisor asks the three men to journey out on the bridge to show him the loose bolts, the painters refuse. The three men are promptly sent home, and a new trio of painters quickly take their jobs. No sooner do the first three men show up for work the following Monday than each is handed their final checks and sent home.

The trial for the construction supervisor of the new bridge charged with violating state safety rules ends in a hung jury. During the superstructure installation, the West Virginia State Safety Commission director charges the bridge's supervisor for failing to comply with state safety law by allowing the steelworkers to work over water without wearing lifejackets. During the three-hour trial, jurors hear testimony that many workers simply refuse to wear lifejackets because the pieces hamper their ability to do their jobs. The jury deliberated less than sixty minutes before announcing its decision.

Just before 12:00noon on Friday, September 12, there is a strike by Painters Local Union 813 at the new bridge site. The strike involves the painters union and the United Painting Contracting Company over workman's compensation and unemployment compensation. The strike halts all construction on the bridge and involves over seventy-five workers. By 2:00pm, the picket lines are down, and work on the bridge resumes.

Despite the recent rash of issues, including a leak in a cofferdam surrounding one of the piers, no less than two union-related work stoppages, the dismissal of three painters who claim that the work being done on the bridge is substandard, a conflict over business taxes, and the trial of the supervisor of construction charged with violating state safety laws, the construction of the new bridge proceeds. Most of the credit is given to the bridge workers who work 8-10 hours a day, seven days a week, so the bridge's steel work can be completed on time. The dedication paid off with the announcement that the pouring of the concrete decks of the span is scheduled to begin the last full week of the month.

Sadly, a second fire hits the downtown area of Point

Pleasant on the last day of the month. The fire, reported around 8:00am, destroys the three-story, 100-year-old building housing the City Insurance Agency and the City Card Shop. The destroyed building is located directly across the street from the buildings that caught fire in January.

The pouring of the bridge deck begins pretty much as scheduled. The concrete for the east side bridge is being supplied by the Wetherholt Construction Company of Henderson. At the same time, the Jenkins Concrete Company of Gallipolis provides the concrete on the west side of the bridge. When asked about the opening of the new bridge, one official is reported to say that it will depend on two things: Mother nature and strikes.

Near the middle of the month, two lawsuits are filed in Kanawha Circuit Court in Charleston seeking $1,000,000 in compensatory damages and $1,000,000 in punitive damages. The plaintiffs in the cases are Lydia Sanders, for the estate of Leo Sanders, and Rosalie McDade on behalf of Alva Lane. Defendants named in the suits are U.S. Steel Corporation and J. E. Greiner. The plaintiffs are represented by the same Charleston law firm that filed the nine lawsuits totaling nearly $19,000,000 in June. Before long, the cases are moved to U.S. District Court.

One of the Painters Local Union 813 falls some 65 feet to the ground this week as he is painting on an upper section of the steel structure. The painter, Roy Stinespring, is sitting in a boatswain's chair suspended from a beam with a rope and pulley when he suddenly begins to fall to the ground. Stinespring lands on a pile of steel rods and is immediately rushed to Cabell-Huntington Hospital. He is listed in serious condition with a leg broken in four places, an arm broken in two places, two crushed jaws, and a host of other injuries. However, this is not the first time Stinespring has fallen from the bridge. Two weeks earlier, he is painting on the structure

156

when the safety belt he is attached to comes untied, causing him to drop some 70 feet into the river. Luckily, he is wearing a lifejacket and is not injured. Stinespring's only loss in the fall are his false teeth. It is reported that he returns to work later that same day.

The first Friday of November brings the news that seven new lawsuits totaling more than $4,000,000 have been filed in U.S. District Court in Columbus, Ohio, on behalf of seven surviving family members who lost loved ones in the bridge collapse. This brings the number of lawsuits filed to ten and the total for reparations to over $5,000,000. The plaintiffs in the latest cases include Hazel Cremeens, wife of Donald Cremeens, John Halliday, Noralyn Head, wife of Bobby Head, and B. K. Higley, father of Forrest Higley. The remaining plaintiffs include Robert Lee, the brother of Thomas Lee, Noel Moore, the father of Ronnie Moore, and Patricia Sims, the wife of the husband and the last of the bodies recovered, Ronald Sims.

One week before Thanksgiving, an earthquake shakes the area. The quake, which hit the area around 8:00pm and registered a 4.7 on the Richter Scale, is centered about 80 miles southeast of Charleston. While there are no reports of damage in the area, one can be confident that such an event causes many people to think about the tragic event of December 15, 1967, and if the earthquake will affect the new bridge's structure.

With a little over a month left in the year, local officials announce that a firm date has been set for the dedication of the new bridge...December 15, two years to the day of the collapse of the Silver Bridge. Just as they did when the Silver Bridge was dedicated in 1928, the dedication ceremonies will begin on the West Virginia side.

Public notice is given that nearly 1,500 tons of scrap steel recovered from the bridge collapse will be sold to the highest bidder at an auction on Wednesday, November 26. The auction is sponsored by the West Virginia Department of Finance and Administration. Shortly after, the state announces that the sale is postponed to give safety experts more time to examine the bridge parts.

With an eye toward sentiment, an ad in the *Athens Messenger* appears that a public auction will be held at a residence in Pennsville, Ohio. Among items to be auctioned off include household furnishings, a player piano and bench, and a brochure from the dedication of the (1928) Silver Bridge.

The day before Thanksgiving, the last of the concrete is poured for the bridge deck. The concrete will need several days to cure. It will be followed by sealing, which will also need several days to dry.

————————————

As excitement grows on both sides of the river surrounding the dedication of the new bridge, the Point Pleasant-Mason County Chamber of Commerce holds a "Name the Bridge" contest. The results indicate that nearly 70% of voters believe the name should be the Silver Memorial Bridge. Other names suggested for the bridge include the Memorial Bridge, Johnson Memorial Bridge, the McClausland Bridge, and the Chief Cornstalk Bridge. Interestingly, local officials want to name the bridge before the dedication ceremony. In contrast, the Silver Bridge was not named until months after its dedication in 1928.

With only a few days remaining before the dedication, reports are circulating on both sides of the Ohio that an unnamed motorist has already driven across the new bridge and was fined $250. The bridge officials deny the story, adding that several workers have crossed the bridge on foot to complete last-minute details as part of the clean-up. Nevertheless, officials stand firm that no one has driven across the bridge. Traditionally, the honor of being the first to drive across the completed bridge is bestowed upon the supervisor of the bridge's superstructure, just as it was in 1928 when Charles Vogel did so at the dedication of the Silver Bridge.

After state and federal inspectors review the bridge's construction one last time, inspectors give a thumbs-up. The final inspection focused mainly on the bridge flooring.

With December 15 the last day for filing claims before the two-year statute of limitations expires, there is a rush of last-minute filings. A suit is filed in U.S. District Court in Baltimore, Maryland, on behalf of thirty-one plaintiffs, each seeking $1,000,000 in damages and $1,000,000 in punitive damages. As expected, the defendants named in the case are U.S. Steel and J. E. Greiner. The plaintiffs claim the bridge was faulty in design and materials. The suit is filed on behalf of the residents of North Carolina, Ohio, Virginia, and West Virginia that died when the Silver Bridge collapsed last year.

Similarly, seven lawsuits have been removed from Kanawha Common Pleas Court and transferred to the same court by the defendants. In two cases, the defendants, U.S. Steel and J. E. Greiner, are being sued by Hennis Freight Lines and McLean Trucking. The plaintiffs are each asking for $150,000 for compensation. William Needham, a driver for the Roadway Express Company, is suing for $250,000. The other four plaintiffs in the filing are suing on behalf of family members, including relatives of Thomas Cantrell, Alonzo Darst, James Maxwell, and Frederick Miller, and are seeking $150,000. Meanwhile, a comparable thing is happening within the West Virginia court system.

In the past few days, no less than eight claims are filed in the West Virginia Court of Claims, including the estates of Albert Adler, Donald Cremeens, Bobby Head, Forrest Higley, Thomas Lee, Ronnie Moore, James Pullen, and Ronald Sims. Each claim seeks $112,000 in damages. Adding to the list is the estate of Gerald McManus, who has filed a claim for $113,000. The McManus filing states that the deceased had an estate of less than $1,000, and funeral costs have caused undue financial stress to his survivors. McManus is survived by a wife and a daughter, age 10.

With the rush of recent filings related to the Silver Bridge collapse, cases now stand at nearly seventy-five, with claims approaching $42,000,000 in alleged damages. Over four dozen cases are filed in the West Virginia Court of Claims totaling over $5,000,000, and approximately twenty-five in state and federal courts totaling nearly $37,000,000. The claims are submitted from survivors, injured persons, and those with property loss. Almost thirty of the filings with the Court of Claims have been filed in the past week. Because the state of West Virginia cannot be sued, claimants must go through the Court of Claims for their portion of the $5,000,000. While most of the claims in the Court of Claims are for the maximum of $100,000 for wrongful death suits, an additional $10,000 may be added for other damages like funeral expenses, etc. If the Court of Claims approves, the process moves to the West Virginia legislature for approval and payment. However, the court will only consider one or two cases. After that, the final decision will be a blanket decision over the remainder of the claims. The current procedure is designed to keep the state immune from being named in a damage lawsuit. Nevertheless, it's apparent that many of those who filed claims in West Virginia have also filed in other state or federal courts and have named U.S. Steel and J. E. Greiner as defendants.

When the dedication day arrives, there is a buzz on both sides of the Ohio. The new bridge is 2,800 feet long and includes five spans, with the middle span measuring around 900 feet. This makes the bridge one of the longest on the Ohio River between Wheeling, West Virginia, and Cincinnati, Ohio. The bridge is designed with no pedestrian walkway. The deck is nearly 70 feet wide and includes four lanes, each approximately 15 feet wide with a center medium of almost three feet. It is believed that around 12,000 cubic yards of concrete are used to construct the bridge, with nearly one-third of that going for the eight-inch thick deck.

Additionally, the superstructure may have required as much as 8,000 tons of steel. In keeping with tradition, the painters coat the structure with three coats of aluminum paint.

The total construction costs, including right-of-ways, approaches, and the like, are approximately $15,000,000. Most striking, the bridge is built in less than two years.

The weather conditions are less than ideal despite the excitement on the dedication day. It is cold, and some even report seeing snow flurries. The weather keeps the crowds that had traveled to the West Virginia side for the ceremony low, around 3,000 to 3,500. The low attendance may also be related to the fact that the dedication is scheduled on a weekday, meaning that most schools are in session and a regular work day for most people in the area. To encourage people from the west shore to attend, one lane of the new bridge is opened for pedestrians to walk over to the ceremony for those that did not want to take the ferry or drive the 40-mile round trip via the Pomeroy Bridge. This will be the only time pedestrians will be allowed on the bridge. However, before the arrival of dignitaries and the official opening of the bridge, the children and teachers of Henderson Grade School walk across the bridge. This gives the group the right to claim that they are the first to walk across the bridge, even before the governors of the two states and the other VIPs.

As pedestrians make their way east across the bridge, signs of the red primer coating are seen peeking through the silver paint. Considering the traditional winter weather in the area, the final paint touch-up may have to wait until spring. More noticeable, however, is the sight to the pedestrians' right, on the opposite shore, of the twisted remains of the former bridge.

In general, the order of the ceremony follows the one used when the Silver Bridge was dedicated forty-one years earlier. However, the activities begin later than the planned 11:00am start. To get the crowd's mind off the weather, it is said that Ohio Governor Jim Rhodes, with some assistance from the Gallia County High School Band, leads those from the left side of the river in an impromptu singalong of "Beautiful Ohio." It is not known if West Virginia Governor Arch Moore countered by encouraging the band from Point Pleasant High School and his constituents to sing "The West Virginia Hills."

Out of respect for those in attendance, Vitus Hartley, Jr., president of the Point Pleasant-Mason County Chamber of Commerce and the master of ceremonies, asks the speakers, including Governors Rhodes and Moore, and keynote speaker, West Virginia Senator Jennings Randolph, to trim their speeches to just a few sentences. The ribbon is cut after the 25-minute ceremony, and the bridge is officially opened. At about the same time that a ferry takes a load of vehicles across the river to Ohio on one final trip, Gov. Moore announces that the new bridge's name will be the Silver Memorial Bridge. The bridge's name will act as a memorial and a path to move forward, a symbolic gesture that life can, and must, go on.

After the speakers have completed their respective speeches, they jump in their cars and are driven to the other side of the bridge. When all parties arrive on the Ohio side of the bridge, they do just as Dr. Holzer and the other dignitaries did at the dedication of the old bridge in 1928…they turn around and drive back to the West Virginia side. Roger Barron, president of the Gallipolis Chamber of Commerce, is master of ceremonies at the luncheon at the Pleasant Point Resort. The special music is provided by the Wahama High School Band.

The Aftermath

In the aftermath of the tragedy, three stories deserve added attention. Moreover, the story of the Silver Bridge would seem incomplete if nothing else is written regarding their outcome. The three stories focus on the impact the bridge's collapse had on future legislation regarding bridge and bridge inspection, the lawsuits brought by the families of the deceased, and the Cantrell lawsuit.

———————

Following his election in 1964, it is recommended to President Lyndon Johnson that a cabinet-level Department of Transportation be created to unify the nearly three dozen departments already operating. Two years later, President Johnson signs a bill into law known as the Department of Transportation Act of 1966. As it initially stood, the bill places the different departments into one of five units such as the Federal Aviation Agency (FAA), the Federal Railroad Administration (FRA), the St. Lawrence Seaway Development Corporation, the National Transportation Safety Board (NTSB), and the Federal Highway Administration (FHA). While the responsibilities of the NTSB are to investigate transportation accidents, determine a probable cause of the accident, and advance recommendations that may prevent future accidents, one of the primary roles of the FHA is to oversee federal funds used for building and maintaining this country's interstate, primary, and secondary roads. It may have been during the interim, when departmental details and responsibilities are being developed and finalized, that the Silver Bridge collapses. Immediately, there were new amendments in the legislation that included several protocols for the Federal Highway Administration. When President Johnson signed the bill on August 24, 1968, the legislation introduced several new programs.

First, a segment of the legislation offered aid to families displaced by new highway construction. Those eligible for federal assistance will receive up to $25,000 to purchase property, up to $5,000 for buying a new home, and reimbursement of 100% of their relocation costs. If renting, the displaced individual or family will receive $1,500. Businesses forced to relocate could receive a lump-sum payment or a percent of their annual net earnings. The legislation included the establishment of a right-of-way fund for states to acquire land for highway construction, funds to encourage the use of mass transportation, and a program to assist states in collecting highway data. Additionally, the act requires any bridge constructed using federal funds to be inspected regularly, forbids bridges built by federal funds to charge tolls, and directs the Department of Transportation to develop bridge safety standards. Most importantly, the act creates the nation's first bridge inspection program.

Nearly a full three years after that horrific night in December 1967, the NTSB issues their final report regarding what they believe to be the cause of the collapse of the Silver Bridge. According to the 140-page report, the failure can be traced to several small, around three millimeters deep, pre-existing pits that had grown around an impurity in the lower half of the steel of eyebar N330. The recesses allow rainwater to pool, causing corrosion and eventually cracking to develop in the metal. Because the eyebars are held in place by a pin and then covered with an endcap, the cracked eyebar could not be seen or detected during the regular inspections or while painting. The lack of redundancy means the bridge would fall if one piece fails. Combined, the convergence of seasonal elements, volume of traffic on the bridge, and the bridge's natural movements over thirty-nine years created the deadly fracture. The report concludes the crack, the thickness of two or three pieces of copy paper, would be nearly impossible to detect without taking the entire suspension apart. There would be no way of seeing these issues short of taking one section of the chain-link suspension and performing an inspection. Even that would compromise the overall integrity of the structure. In the end, the NTSB blamed neither the designers nor the builders. This conclusion will go a long way in deciding the pending lawsuits.

Further legislation enacted in the spring of 1971 adds teeth to the historic highway bill. First, it establishes National Bridge Inspection Standards for inspecting bridges and a federal and state program to train employees to implement the standards. A bridge inspector's manual and a comprehensive training course are also a part of the legislation. To encourage a working relationship between the federal and state levels of government, each state's department of transportation (DOT) will shoulder the responsibility to inspect all highway bridges on public roads that are fully or partially located within each state's boundaries. The exception will be for bridges owned by federal agencies. Lastly, the legislation establishes a national bridge inventory and mandates that bridge inspections be conducted at least every two years.

When the last celebrations surrounding the new bridge conclude on December 15, 1969, court records indicate no less than seventy-four lawsuits had been filed in various state and federal courts. The first of these filings came nineteen months earlier as the administrator of Transcon truck driver Leo Blackman's estate filed suit in Kanawha Circuit Court in Charleston. Filed by Blackman's sister, the lawsuit seeks $1,000,000 in damages and an additional $1,000,000 for punitive and exemplary damages. The defendants in the case are the J. E. Greiner Company, who designed the plans for the Silver Bridge, U.S. Steel, who provided the steel, and the U.S. Government.

On the same day of the Blackman filing, four additional suits totaling $8,000,000 are filed by Clara Towe, Nancy Bennett, Marie Cundiff, and Judy Mabe. Additional lawsuits are not filed until nearly two months *before* the new bridge is opened. The plaintiffs in these cases are the administrators of the estates of Melvin Cantrell, Cecil Counts, and Marvin Wamsley. Cantrell and Counts were among the first group of

166

persons who died the night of the bridge's collapse. Wamsley's body was recovered west of the Ohio tower on December 19. Unlike the previous filings, the plaintiffs in these cases file their suits in the West Virginia Court of Claims. In each of the newest cases, the defendant is the West Virginia State Road Commission, and each plaintiff seeks $112,000 in damages.

Around November 7, three additional lawsuits are filed in the West Virginia Court of Claims against the State Road Commission. The plaintiff in one case is the estate of Donna Casey, and the claim is for $112,000. The other two claims are for $1,575 and $1,350 for the loss of two cars damaged when the bridge collapsed and are filed by Nationwide Mutual Insurance Company. This brings the total claims to date against the West Virginia State Road Commission to six.

Neary a month later, an additional claim was filed in the Court of Claims for $100,000 on behalf of the estate of Gerald McManus. In addition, the administrator of his estate has filed a lawsuit in Common Pleas Court for $250,000. Before long, there are seven additional suits filed. Among the suits, each seeking $125,000, are the estates of Thomas Cantrell, Alonzo Darst, James Maxwell, and Frederick Miller. In addition, Hennis Trucking and McLean Trucking are asking for $150,000 for the loss of equipment and cargo. Finally, Roadway Express employee, William Needham, has filed a $250,000 suit, claiming total and permanent disability from the injuries he received the night of the collapse. Shortly after, the plaintiffs in the last seven cases are notified that their lawsuits have been transferred from Kanawha County courts to U.S. District Court.

As the first anniversary of the opening of the Silver Memorial Bridge arrives, there is a rush of lawsuits filed to beat the two-year deadline for filing a suit. The records indicate that at the close of business on Monday, December 15, 1969, there are seventy-four suits and claims totaling nearly $42,000,000. Claims against the West Virginia State Road Commission are forty-seven, totaling over $5,300,000. Of the forty-seven claims, over thirty of them came during the last few days of filing. The remaining twenty-seven cases, totaling nearly $37,000,000, are filed in state and federal courts, including Maryland, Ohio, and West Virginia. The plaintiffs in the seventy-four claims and suits are filed by the survivors of the victims of the collapse, injured persons, and those who suffered property damage through loss of cars, trucks, etc. In the cases filed with the Court of Claims, the plaintiffs are basing their claims on a moral obligation of the state of West Virginia to grant the claims. In cases petitioning over the $110,000 limit, the plaintiff must present "provable damages" such as funeral expenses, etc., to receive additional awards. The state limit in the latter case is $10,000. If claims in the West Virginia Court of Claims are granted, the grant amount goes to the West Virginia legislature for a straight yes or no vote. This process exists because the state is immune from being named a defendant in a damage suit.

On April 20, 1970, the lawsuits filed in the Southern District of Maryland and the Southern District of Ohio are transferred to the Southern District of West Virginia. While the total number of cases with a venue change is 56, it is discovered that several cases are duplicates and have been filed in more than one district.

The much-awaited final findings of the NTSB are issued three years and one day (December 16, 1970) after the collapse of the Silver Bridge. After merging the results of the three committees first appointed on December 20, 1967, to review the bridge's design and history, question witnesses, and conduct a structural analysis, the NTSB issues a 140-page document. They cite the cause of the collapse as a fracture of the lower limb of eyebar N330 at joint C13N. Further, the report states that the fracture grew due to stress corrosion and fatigue. In part, the report reads…

> *"The Safety Board finds that the cause of the bridge collapse was the cleavage fracture in the lower limb of the eye of eyebar 330 at joint C13N of the north eyebar suspension chain in the Ohio side span. The fracture of the structure was the result of the joint action of stress*

corrosion and corrosion fatigue." (*Accident Highway Report, Collapse of U. S. Highway 35 Bridge, Point Pleasant, West Virginia, December 15, 1967, pg. 9*)

Additionally, the Safety Board lists three causes that contributed to the collapse, including the unknown element at the time the bridge was built of stress corrosion and corrosion fatigue, the inaccessibility of some of the eyebars for inspection, and the absence of any known method to inspect the eyebars short of dismantling the suspension system. Noticeably absent from the report is the centering of negligence on the part of the bridge designers, the company that built the superstructure, or the owners or caretakers of the bridge: the state of West Virginia.

Despite the conclusions offered, there seems to be little or no action surrounding the lawsuits for the next three years.

In March 1973, a trial date is set for the lawsuits pending in the West Virginia Court of Claims. Of the 56 suits, forty-four are wrongful death suits totaling $4,900,000, eight personal injury claims for $950,000, and four property suits totaling around $500,000. In nearly every case, the claimants cite negligence in the bridge's original design, negligence by the state of West Virginia to properly examine the bridge when it was purchased in 1941, and negligence on the part of the state to properly inspect and maintain the bridge.

Late that summer, the West Virginia Court of Claims warns that it will dismiss the claims of all the 56 claimants unless there is some movement on the cases. The court claims that the lawsuits have been on the court's books for several years, and if there is no action in the next 30-days or so, the files will be closed. Before long, two of the three defendants in the lawsuits, the Greiner Company and U.S. Steel, settle forty-one of the fifty-six cases out of court. The Greiner Company will pay a total of $200,000 to the claimants, and U.S. Steel will pay $750,000. The exact amount to each plaintiff will be determined at a later date. One plaintiff, the family of Thomas Cantrell, later reports that they received a total of $14,000, and about half of that went toward legal fees.

Of the three charges levied against the U.S. government, two are dismissed. The government is found guilty of the third charge, namely, the federal government's activities in and around the Kanawha and Ohio River banks between 1927 and 1967. Specifically, the lawyers for the plaintiffs cite two events that occur after the bridge is completed in 1928, and both, they contend, led to or contributed to the ultimate collapse of the bridge. In 1937, the Gallipolis Lock and Dam is completed 14 miles downstream from the Silver Bridge. This dam raises the river's elevation between 15-18 feet above the normal pool stage at the Silver Bridge. The building of a 26-foot flood wall at Point Pleasant also played a critical role in raising the river from its normal pool stage.

In early fall, the West Virginia Attorney General reiterates the belief that the state is not responsible for the deaths following the bridge's collapse. And since the claimants have settled with those responsible for the design and construction of the bridge, the lawsuits should be treated as complete, or at least partial, settlements. Meanwhile, a court date to officially begin the trial in the Court of Claims is set for spring 1974. Lawyers on both sides of the courtroom expect the trial to last several months since the case will be heard by three part-time judges, who can preside only 2 or 3 days each month.

Because of a delay, witness testimony in the trial does not begin in earnest until July 1974. But before the opening, it is decided that rather than try the cases one by one, two test cases will be chosen in particular. These two cases will determine the fate of the remaining cases. If the West Virginia State Road Commission is found not to be liable, the proceedings will end immediately. Conversely, the results will be forwarded to the West Virginia legislature if the SRC is found guilty. After that, the cases will proceed, and the damages awarded. The "test cases" are the lawsuits filed by Margaret Cantrell and the one filed by the survivors of James White. Before the cases go to trial, two additional claims for wrongful death are filed in the Court of Claims, each in the amount of $110,000. The two filings involve the estates of Kathy Byus and Maxine Turner, the two missing bodies.

For fourteen days, between July 1974 and April 1975, the three judges presiding over the cases, Judges John Garden, George Wallace, Jr., and Daniel Ruley, Jr., hear testimony from several witnesses, including state of West Virginia witnesses Charles Scheffey of the NTSB, Joseph Jones, West Virginia State Highway Engineer for Construction, Chester Comstock, from the firm of Modjeski and Masters, state road commission workers, scientists, and engineering professionals. Testifying for the plaintiffs are bridge experts Abba Lichenstein, Dr. Istvan Tuba, and Dr. Charles Schalt. On May 28, 1976, after nearly forty-eight years to the day the Silver Bridge was dedicated and almost eight and one-half years after it collapsed, the three judges issue their 39-page opinion. The judges rule that there is no way that the State Road Commission could have anticipated or foreseen the fracture in the exercise of standard care of the bridge. Subsequently, the court exonerates the state of West Virginia of any negligence or liability, and no damages will be awarded to the plaintiffs. The same principle is applied to the fifteen cases against the federal government. Similar to the report of the NTSB issued five years earlier, the court rules nobody is to blame.

––––––––––––

It might be said that the narrative involving Melvin Cantrell and his family begins on Monday, December 18, 1967, and does not end until seven years to the day after his funeral, December 18, 1974.

In attendance at the funeral service for 40-year-old Melvin Cantrell on December 18, 1967, is a freelance reporter from the *Cleveland Plain Dealer*. A few days later, a story appears in the northeast Ohio newspaper describing the scene at the funeral service and some sorted details about Cantrell and his life. The article says that Cantrell is married, has seven children, worked for the West Virginia Sate Road Commission, and lives a modest life. Above all, the initial article focuses on the impact of Cantrell's passing on his family. The article earns the reporter a cash award from the newspaper.

After conferring with an editor at the newspaper, the reporter returns to the area several months later to do a follow-up feature on the Cantrell family. This time, however, the reporter brings along a photographer with him. Neither the reporter nor the photographer call and make arrangements for the interview, and Mrs. Cantrell is not around. As the reporter speaks with the minor children, the photographer roams around the home, taking nearly fifty pictures. During the 60 to 90 minutes they are in the house, the two men gather material for the article. A few days later, an article and five accompanying pictures appear in the August 4, 1968, edition of the *Sunday Magazine* of the Plain Dealer regarding the reporter's visit. However, the article contains several admitted inaccuracies regarding the Cantrell family, most notably, the family's abject poverty, the conditions inside the home, and the children's clothing. It may have been that the reporter was trying to illustrate the impact of the bridge collapse on the lives of certain people in the Point Pleasant area.

Regardless, Mrs. Cantrell and her four minor children sue the newspaper for defamation and the "false light" theory of invasion of privacy. The plaintiffs believe the article brings them embarrassment, shame, and public humiliation. Moreover, they believe the article communicates something that is factually untrue, seems to convey a false impression, or is highly offensive to a reasonable person. In addition, the Cantrells ask the court for punitive damages.

When the case makes it to trial in 1972, the reporter is no longer associated with the newspaper. Beyond the reporter not being asked to testify at the trial, the newspaper contends that they had no knowledge of the inaccuracies contained in the article. At the conclusion of the trial, and before the case goes to the jury, the judge removes the plaintiff's demand for punitive damages because the plaintiff's lawyers had failed to present evidence that the inaccuracies and flaws found in the

172

article stemmed from malice on the part of the reporter and his accomplice. Subsequently, the defendants move for a directed verdict, which the judge denies. In time, the jury finds the defendants, the newspaper and its parent company, Forest Publishing, guilty of invading a family's privacy by publishing the error-laced article and awards compensatory damages to the Cantrells. Proving that the newspaper showed a blatant disregard for the truth in publishing the story, the court awards Margaret Cantrell and her family $60,000.

In 1973, the defendants appeal the case to the U.S. Court of Appeals for the Sixth District (Cincinnati). They overturn the lower court's decision. Specifically, the judges believe that the freedom of the press overrides a person's right to privacy. Moreover, the judges believe the lower court should have granted the defendant's motion for a directed verdict. In their opinion, the higher court believes there is a natural and inevitable interaction between a person's right to privacy and the public's right to know.

But in 1974, the Supreme Court reverses the decision of the U.S. Court of Appeals and rules in favor of the Cantrells. In an 8-1 decision, the high court believes the evidence is sufficient to show the paper had acted with actual malice and that the reporter knowingly wrote the story even though it contained several false statements. Moreover, the court believed that though the reporter was considered a freelance reporter, the newspaper was guilty because the reporter had been acting on the newspaper's behalf.

The Numbers

With a great deal of the book behind us and, quite possibly, the most valuable chapter still ahead, this may be an excellent time to quickly review the numbers. This said, consider…

0	number of the nine survivors pulled from the wreckage of the Silver Bridge that are still alive today
1	college student on the bridge at the time of the collapse (R. Moore)
2	months youngest child to pass away when bridge falls (Kimberly Byus); WV State Road Commission employees (Me. Cantrell, D. Northup); workers for Marietta Manufacturing Company (D. Cremeens, A. Lane); workers for City of Point Pleasant (J. Meadows, V. Turner); workers for Merry Stone Company (A. Darst, F. Higley); residents of Virginia (J. Blackman, R. Towe)
3	teachers on the bridge (D. Taylor, G. Taylor, and J. White); workers at Goodyear Plant (A. Adler, R. Head, R. Sims); workers for NYC Railroad (J. Pullen, F. Miller, P. Scott); residents of North Carolina (J. Bennett, H. Cundiff, D. Mabe); bridges under the state of Ohio care (Chester/Newell Bridge, Ft. Steuben Bridge, Pomeroy Bridge)
4	parents that lost a child when bridge collapsed (Boggs, Byus 2, Meadows, Mayes); joint funeral services (Byus, Meadows, Smith, Wedge)
5	the number of children under the age of fourteen that passed away from the bridge's

collapse (K. Boggs, Ka. Byus, Ki. Byus, D. Mayes, T. Meadows; days L. Sanders died before his birthday (December 20); tractor-trailers on the bridge the evening of the collapse (Hennis, McLean, Roadways 2, and Transcon); those with January birthdays (D. Casey, D. Cremeens, F. Higley, A. Lane, D. Mayes); cents per person to walk across the Silver Bridge before the tolls were removed

7   drivers on the bridge who lived in North Carolina (J. Bennett, H. Cundiff, S. Ellis, W. Edmondson, G. Mabe, W. Needham, W. Nunn)

8   most bodies recovered on one day, December 20; vehicles heading east on the bridge the night of the collapse; dams on the Ohio River in 1967 between Pittsburgh and the Gallipolis Dam (Emsworth, Dashields, Montgomery, New Cumberland, Pike Island, Belleview, Racine, and the Gallipolis)

9   survivors taken to area hospitals the night of the bridge's collapse (H. Boggs, Margaret Cantrell, W. Edmondson, S. Ellis, J. Fishel, W. Needham, F. Nunn, P. Scott, F. Wamsley)

10   number of bridges on the Ohio River in 1967 that are south of Pittsburgh and north of Huntington, and owned by either Ohio or West Virginia (Chester/Newell-East Liverpool, Market Street, Weirton-Ft. Steuben, Ft. Henry, Bellaire, New Martinsville, Hi Carpenter, Memorial, Mason-Pomeroy, and Silver Bridge)

11	funerals held on December 20
12	veterans on either the main or side spans of the bridge at the time of the collapse (T. Cantrell, D. Cremeens, H. Cundiff, R. Head, F. Higley, A. Lane, T. Lee, J. Meadows, J. Pullen, R. Sims, L. Sanders, J. White)
13	number of months F. Higley spent in Vietnam; Pickens cab number L. Sanders was driving the night of collapse
14	January, 1968, the day Darlene "Deenie" Mayes would have celebrated her 14th birthday
15	December, 1967, the day of the Silver Bridge collapse; December, 1969, dedication of the new (Memorial Bridge)
17	*Days That Changed America* as a result of the bridge collapse
19	residents of West Virginia (Byus 3, Me. Cantrell, C. Counts, A. Duff, Meadows 2, N. Nibert, D. Northup, L. Sanders, D. Taylor, G. Taylor, M. Turner, V. Turner, Marvin Wamsley, L. Wedge, P. Wedge, J. White)
20	July, 1928, first couple married on the bridge (B. Balch and G. Stephenson); approximate number of vehicles on the middle span of the bridge when it fell
21	approximate number of funerals that took place in the area between December 18 and December 31

22   residents of Ohio that perish in the collapse (A. Adler, Boggs 2, D. Casey, T. Cantrell, H. Cremeens, A. Darst, J. Hawkins, R. Head, F. Higley, A. Lane, T. Lee, J. Maxwell, D. Mayes, G. McManus, F. Miller, R. Moore, J. Pullen, R. Sims, C. Smith, O. Smith, M. Sturgeon); funerals that were held in the course eleven days; the number of different cemeteries in the area where those that passed away from the collapse are buried; number of cars on the bridge at the time of the collapse (7 Fords, 5 Chevrolets, 4 Pontiacs, 2 Ramblers, and one each Buick, Dodge, Oldsmobile, Volkswagen)

24   ministers that conducted a funeral between December 18 and December 31; one minister officiated at three funerals in the course of three days; one minister officiated at two services on one day and in a matter of hours of each other

27   approximate distance in miles of the Racine Dam from the Silver Bridge

28   October, 1928, Hi Carpenter (St. Marys) Bridge opens for traffic

29   vehicles heading west on the bridge at the time of the collapse (6 on the Ohio approach, 11 on the Ohio span, and 12 on the middle span)

30   May, 1928, Silver Bridge dedicated, opens for traffic; approximate number of tugboats pushing barges that are forced to moor until wreckage site is cleared

30.3	distance from the water to the bridge deck of the Silver Bridge during the 1937 flood
31	vehicles on the bridge at the time of the collapse (23 cars, 5 tractor-trailers, 2 dump trucks, and one pick-up); last day in December that the Corps. of Engineers work fulltime in the area of the bridge
35	cents, for a one-way fare on the Doodlebug train from Point Pleasant to Kanauga; the cost to ride the train from Point Pleasant to Gallipolis is 50 cents; total distance in miles that river traffic is stopped on both sides of the Ohio River
37	total vehicles on the bridge the evening of the collapse (24 vehicles went into the water, 7 dropped on Ohio bank, and 6 remained in the wreckage of the bridge)
39	average age of individuals (less children) on the bridge at time of collapse; the length in pages of the final decision rendered by the West Virginia Court of Claims in 1976
40	years of marriage for Charles and Oma Smith
44	number of children under the age of 10 years that lost a parent in the bridge collapse, number of bodies recovered
46	total lives lost when the bridge collapsed
50	the amount of prize money given to the best decorated car from each side of the river at the 1928 bridge dedication

56	total claims filed against the West Virginia State Road Commission; includes 44 wrongful death suits, 8 personal injury claims, and 4 for property damage
62.72	level of the Ohio River at Point Pleasant during the historic 1937 flood
63.11	the length in feet and inches of the eyebar 330
64	age of the oldest person to pass away from the bridge's collapse (Oma Smith); number of people on the bridge in 37 vehicles when the bridge collapsed
70	distance from the water to the bridge deck of the Silver Bridge during normal river levels
80	feet, the distance that Delno Jackson travels as he jumps off the new bridge and into the waters of the Ohio River rather than get hit by a passing motorist; Jackson is doing touch-up painting on the bridge at the time
120	distance in miles the body of Denzil Taylor is recovered from the site of the collapse
140	length in pages of the final report of the NTSB issued in December 1970 citing the cause of the collapse as a fracture of the lower limb of eyebar 330 at joint C13N, fracture grew as a result of stress corrosion and fatigue
148	the number of eyebars installed on the Silver Bridge

150	days from when the bridge collapsed until the day the body of Thomas Cantrell is recovered
265	approximate distance in river miles from the head waters of the Ohio River in Pittsburgh to the Silver Bridge
300	estimate of how many feet of the Silver Bridge still remains in the Ohio River at Point Pleasant
330	the number of the eyebar (N330) found to be faulty
1,000	yards, the approximate distance the Roadway truck had floated downstream which contained the recovered body of R. Towe
1909	year that Dr. C. Holzer settles in Gallipolis
1925	year the Gallia County Ohio River Bridge Company is incorporated
1927	March, drilling for bridge piers begins
1928	decision to paint the bridge with an aluminum-based silver paint
1937	the state of West Virginia purchases Hi Carpenter Bridge; the year of the great flood
1941	the state of West Virginia purchases the Silver Bridge just over $1,000,000
1952	tolls removed from Silver Bridge
1966	June, Silver Bridge piers hit by runaway barges

1977	July, inspectors find countless defects in the welding of the new bridge, two lanes of the new bridge are closed for approximately three months
2,339	pages of compiled records during nine months of Court of Claims hearings
4,000	cost per day in dollars to rent clamshell cranes
5,053	pounds, weight of eyebar N330
100,000	estimated cost in dollars for the first week of search and recovery
898,096	the total in dollars it cost to construct the Silver Bridge, of this $862,341 is attributed to construction
9,000,000	estimated amount in dollars to construct new four-lane bridge over the Ohio River near Point Pleasant/Gallipolis
14,600,000	dollars, final cost to construct the Silver Memorial Bridge

The Lessons

As another anniversary quickly approaches, the memories are still fresh in the minds of some on both sides of the river. Most remember where they were when they heard the news of the collapse and what they were doing at the time. They remember how their tiny community was suddenly inundated with tv cameras, reporters, government workers, and gawkers, and how private lives swiftly became public ones. They remember being physically and emotionally separated from loved ones and friends on the opposite shore, leaving extra early to get to work and arriving home long after sundown, and waiting hours for a ferry to transport them across the quarter-mile river. Most of all, they remember their reaction upon hearing who had died when the bridge fell into the Ohio River and who was missing.

Death was not selective on December 15, 1967. That particular night it took males and females, young and old, locals and those merely passing through the area. Those that perished that cold December night were family members, neighbors, and co-workers. They were mothers and fathers with young children at home and looking forward to a festive Christmas. Among those names appearing on the chalkboard were young kids who had their whole life ahead of them, middle-aged workers who knew what it was like to do an honest day's work for an honest day's pay, and veterans who had served their country with honor. One loss is traumatic, but 46 of them at once?

Granted, others died in 1967, including poets Carl Sandburg and Dorothy Parker, stage and screen stars Vivian Leigh and Spencer Tracy, astronauts Virgil Grissom and Paul Chaffee, physicist J. Robert Oppenheimer, singer Otis Redding, entrepreneur Leon Leonwood (L.L.) Bean, baseball star Jimmie Foxx, and Carl Washkansky. History noted their passing. As for those forty-six lives lost when the Silver Bridge fell, they never had anything published, acted in a movie, circled the Earth, made a noted invention, played major league baseball, or created a clothing empire. Those that passed that night were teachers and coaches, railroad workers and truck drivers, cabbies, and students. These were everyday people like you and me. They were church-goers who happened to be at the wrong place at the wrong time. They didn't ask to have their names, occupations, or marital status revealed to the world. It just happened.

And yet, their lives have impacted more lives than they will ever know. As it turns out, their lives have saved thousands, even millions, over the years. They unknowingly changed the course of American highway and bridge safety, and the tragedy created a ripple effect nationwide. The passing of those forty-six individuals raised awareness and provided fertile ground for future engineers and bridge builders. Additionally, the tragic death of those lives ushered in federal legislation that focused on bridge safety, training for bridge inspectors, and regular inspections of all local, state, and federal bridges. Above all, it brought attention to the national issue of an aging infrastructure, especially structurally-deficient bridges and the need to regularly allocate resources to repair and replace them. The lives of the individuals who passed away should not be forgotten, their contributions overlooked, and their sacrifices ignored. The lives they gave are the legacy they leave.

The Silver Bridge collapse hit both communities hard, economically, emotionally, and socially. However, there is much more to the story than longer travel times, shopping inconveniences, and the opening of a new bridge. Moreover, the not-so-glowing media coverage sometimes seemed to focus more on the area's culture and way of life than the collapse itself. This only added to the nation's perception of the area. But in typical fashion, those on both sides of the river did more than step up. They took giant steps to work through the economic, social, and emotional challenges. In doing so, they set an example for dealing with pain and loss. Subsequently, we must not, and cannot, overlook the not-so-obvious lessons that came from this tragedy.

For starters, there is a lesson here on the importance of cooperation.

As the initial shock and confusion of the collapse inflicted its pain on the community that terror-filled night and local residents began to grapple with what had happened, the search and recovery process immediately shifted to the "professionals." Within hours of the collapse, members of both the Henderson and the Huntington Units of the Coast Guard began arriving on the scene. They were followed shortly after that by members of the Corps. of Engineers. Each had their job to do.

The Coast Guard assumed responsibility for all surface activities, controlling river traffic, and searching for victims downstream. Within a short time, westbound river traffic on the Kanawha River was stopped at the Winfield Locks, and all barge traffic on the Ohio was immediately halted from the Racine Locks south to the Gallipolis Dam, a distance of some 35 miles.

Similarly, the Corps' efforts focused on all matters about the bridge, including the later removal of vehicles and bridge steel from the river, obstacles that would impede commercial navigation, and oversight of underwater activity and contract operations. The list of organizations contracted by the Corps. to provide additional support were deep-sea divers from Connecticut, barge-mounted cranes, derrick boats, towboats, and launches. Additionally, nearly ten dams along the Ohio River between the headwaters of the river in Pittsburgh and the site of the collapse are told to make adjustments to reduce the volume and flow of water downstream. By Sunday, December 17, full-scale recovery efforts began in earnest.

Equally impressive was the collective effort at the federal level to re-establish local and regional commerce and transportation over the river and assist those in the area to begin looking to the future. Less than five days after the tragedy, President Lyndon Johnson directed the newly established NTSB to investigate the bridge's collapse and determine the cause. With economic losses estimated at $1,000,000 a month to the area, President Johnson calls the failure a national disaster and the absence of a bridge a national emergency. Subsequently, the president orders federal and state governments to begin working on a new bridge to re-connect the two states. In addition to announcing federal monies estimated to be over $6,000,000, President Johnson vows the new bridge will be built in half the time it usually takes a bridge to be constructed.

Above all, the specialized work of federal leaders in the first few hours and days following the tragedy allowed state and local leaders time to come to terms with the physical pain of the disaster and the emotional grief. And once the immediate chaos and confusion became manageable, state leaders on both sides of the river began doing their part in the united effort.

State officials began inspecting all bridges along the river, starting with the Chester/Newell Bridge connecting Chester/Newell, West Virginia, and East Liverpool, Ohio. Specifically, the declaration included the bridge at St. Marys that was constructed using eyebars. As for the members of the West Virginia State Police and the Ohio Highway Patrol, they assumed the responsibility of collecting eye-witness accounts of the tragedy. Moreover, members of the West Virginia State Police are on nearby boats to record the type of vehicle recovered and the number of bodies inside. After a body is recovered and taken to the West Virginia shore, it is given to members of the West Virginia State Police, who not only place the body in an awaiting ambulance but accompany it to the morgue. As parts of the bridge are recovered, the location of the recovered piece is noted by a representative of the West Virginia State Road Commission, numbered, and loaded onto waiting barges.

Above all, one cannot overlook the ongoing involvement of local leaders and people from both sides of the river and around the region in the cooperative efforts following the bridge's collapse. Within minutes of the disaster, the townspeople on both sides of the river rescued survivors and recovered bodies. Less than two hours had passed before local volunteers from West Virginia and Ohio units of the Red Cross began setting up sleeping accommodations for workers. By the time the governors from the two states appeared on the scene around 10:00pm on December 15, food had been donated, taken to local churches, and delivered to workers. Additionally, food canteens staffed by local volunteers were established on both the east and west shores of the river. By the end of the first week after the tragedy, countless toy drives and monies were collected for the children who had lost a parent in the collapse.

During the five weekends of dragging in the early months of January and February 1968, volunteers from surrounding states also took part. They were housed thanks to local contributions. As members of local organizations in the two communities became involved, students followed by organizing book drives, donating club funds, and searching the banks along the river. Local and regional newspapers utilized their public position and circulation to keep the people abreast of meetings, where they could get assistance, the progress of recovery and rebuilding, and, most importantly, those still missing by providing up-to-date and objective reporting. Above all, local leaders made a concerted and cooperative effort to allow people to get involved in the short-term recovery efforts and provide them a long-term path to invest their time and effort when they were emotionally ready to do so.

The two communities that literally existed at opposite ends of the bridge could have worked independently, but they did not. If there were differences, they quickly disappeared, and trivial things became just that…trivial things. It was not West Virginians and Ohioans, Mountaineers and Buckeyes, Democrats and Republicans, or even Christians and non-Christians. It was neighbor helping neighbor and friend helping friend. The "me" quickly became the "we." The volunteers did not step up because they had to; instead, they rose to the occasion because they wanted to.

The lesson in cooperation following the collapse of the Silver Bridge cannot, and must not, be understated. In the hours, days, and weeks following the tragedy, the leaders at all levels of government did not allow the disaster to lead to widespread economic destabilization or social defragmentation. On the contrary, even though the dust had yet to settle from the tragedy, the collective work was set in motion as the federal government addressed the immediate needs and allowed state and local leaders to tackle secondary ones. Moreover, the 17 days the federal government spent addressing the urgent needs of the situation permitted local leaders the time they needed to arrange for the proper handing over of duties. Instead of rolling over upon the exit of the Corps. of Engineers and the others on the last day of December 1967, the cooperation at all levels allowed state and local leaders the time to take stock of the situation, assess needs, allocate resources, and assign local responsibilities. Subsequently, the cooperative efforts at recovery and rebuilding did not miss a beat!

A second and equally important lesson from the bridge collapse centers on the importance of community following a tragedy.

Ask any group of people that's experienced a debilitating loss from a flood, a major fire, a hurricane, or other disaster, and they will tell you that the loss has the potential to do one of two things. First, the tragedy has the immediate capacity to create feelings of being alone and isolated, that no one can relate to the pain. Beyond the emotional aspects, there are the physical aspects like lethargy and anxiety. While one loss of life is one too many, losing several lives at once can multiply the emotional and physical factors. Last but not least, it can be said there is a social dimension to a tragedy. It can divide friends, create communal differences, and even tear at the very fabric of family life.

Beyond providing a sense of security following a disaster, a tragedy can create feelings of togetherness and bonding. Moreover, a tragedy has the potential to draw people together, make friends out of strangers, and established relationships even stronger while creating a sense of oneness and unity because of a common struggle. Likewise, tragedies have been known to develop an understanding of connectedness, togetherness, and a feeling that we're all in this together. Finally, as strange as it may sound, a tragedy has the inertia to empower, inspire, motivate, and energize. And no one knew better the importance of maintaining and nurturing a sense of community following the bridge collapse than John (Andy) Wilson, the Civil Defense director on the West Virginia side of the river, and his counterpart on the Ohio side, John Epling.

Their intentional efforts are worthy of the highest praise.

Initially, the two men focused their efforts on people instead of projects. Wilson and Epling were fully aware of the trauma of loss that the townspeople felt. Consequently, they allowed people time to grieve and mourn at their own pace. It was apparent that the two directors thought it was more critical for them to begin rebuilding lives than rebuilding the communities. When the time was right, they implemented a systematic approach to get people involved in the search and recovery process.

First, Wilson and Epling gave townspeople on both sides of the river a reason to get involved. After all, the vast majority of those that lost loved ones when the bridge collapsed were local people. In fact, upwards of 90% of those that perished had family in the immediate area. Next, the two leaders endeavored to make people feel valued, their talents needed, and their contributions crucial to the recovery and rebuilding. Following this, Wilson and Epling provided an avenue for people to channel grief into action by inviting people to share their time and individual gifts to supply needs…and many did.

Two local Point Pleasant men made their contribution by installing a radio antenna on the roof of the Pleasant County Courthouse, despite having to do so in the middle of the night in a sleet storm. For those not able to contribute physically, they were asked to contribute empty bleach and milk containers to be used to mark the location of submerged vehicles. Others open their homes as sleeping quarters for those volunteers from out of state who showed up to assist in dragging operations. Still others, like Sandy Dunn, the mother of five children, including a set of triplets, cooked spaghetti for the workers while others donated money. Some volunteered their time during the dragging weekends in January and February, including Apple Grove resident and Navy seaman QM3, John Ball. He was home on leave from Vietnam when the tragedy occurred and spent much of his thirty-one days of "r-and-r" on the river. And for those unable to contribute physically or financially, they became involved in the effort by simply praying. These intentional avenues of involvement developed by Wilson and Epling gave people on both sides of the river a reason to get up in the mornings. More, it became a powerful healing tool for many on both sides of the river and a reminder that the two communities are one community, joined through a tragedy that claimed 46 lives.

Equally important are the unintentional consequences of Wilson and Epling's effort to maintain community in the face of disaster. The efforts at recovery brought people from various economic, educational, and social backgrounds together for a common purpose. As townspeople began working side by side with others, they became closer. Friendships were founded, and trust was created. The sharing of everyday trials became a bridge to recovery while acting as a reminder that all hurt when one hurts. Restaurants became more than a place to get a meal. They became places to share emotions and gain spiritual nourishment. Over a simple cup of coffee, people found support, encouragement, and regeneration.

Similarly, churches became more than a place to worship. They became places to express grief and receive empowerment, a place to be fully human, tears and all. Likewise, community meetings became places where people were assured that they were not alone, that joys and sorrows are shared ones, and a place where people are reminded that resiliency is key to a brighter tomorrow.

At a time when Point Pleasant and Gallipolis could have suffered irreparable harm following the bridge's collapse, economically and socially, the efforts of Wilson and Epling to maintain community and further oneness and unity through the involvement of townspeople are noteworthy. In the end, the actions of these two men did much to help their respective communities. Beyond providing people a purpose and a path for involvement in the recovery, the two men were able to rebuild lives.

A third lesson one can draw from the events surrounding the collapse of the Silver Bridge centers on the endearing quality of compassion.

Undoubtedly, things seemed unreal those first few hours and days following the collapse. The news about the failure was not in another state or even a far-off country. The tragedy was here and in a place few knew of or could locate on a map. It was here, along the banks of the Ohio River, and it had happened to people on both sides of a bridge that most had never heard of, let alone traveled. At a moment's notice, lives were suddenly turned upside down. Thomas Cantrell, a distributing agent for a local newspaper, was now part of the national news story. State Road Commission workers Melvin Cantrell and Darius Northup passed away on the very bridge they may have worked to maintain.

Moreover, the people they saw on tv being interviewed or written about in newspapers were not hundreds of miles away. Instead, these were co-workers they had worked beside for years. Those that lost their lives that cold December night were former classmates and people they had fished or hunted with among the hills and valleys of West Virginia and Ohio. These were individuals whose kids played with their kids, worshipped where they worshipped, and shopped where they shopped. Beyond being a mass tragedy, these were 46 individual lives. Suddenly gone were parents with young children, individuals that waited on them at the restaurant or the grocery store. This tragic event crept into every home and heart in Point Pleasant and Gallipolis. People at one end of the bridge could identify with the heartache and sense of loss happening at the other end of the bridge. There was relatedness because everybody knew somebody on the bridge that night.

Consequently, the event's magnitude caused most to become emotionally numb and confused. Not only were individuals struggling to come to terms with what had happened but so were their family members, friends, neighbors, and co-workers. The collapse's physical, social, and emotional ramifications were broad and cannot be understated. People were on edge and fragile.

As expected, individuals were in different places emotionally following the collapse. Some were angry, others were in shock, but most were confused and felt helpless. A sudden loss and the trauma connected with it will do that, even to the emotionally strong. Additionally, most did not know which way to turn or what to do next, let alone help others. Beyond the tragedy, ancillary aspects needed an immediate response. There were essentials to be met, and individuals needed to be fed, housed, and cared for emotionally. While most struggled to come to terms with what had happened, others on both sides of the river jumped into action in the temporary absence of community-based help.

Even as they are working through their own emotions, local clergy and nurses are providing comfort to families called to the National Guard Armory to identify the bodies of loved ones. Beyond being a place to worship, individuals showed up at churches to donate food, prepare it, and deliver it to workers. People went to praying, not only for those that lost loved ones but for the local leaders and workers. Phone calls suddenly meant more, and cards of sympathy and support became tools of empathy and empowerment. Every word spoken to another on the street was founded on concern, caring, and kindness. When words like "let me know if you need something" or "how are you doing?" were voiced, they were honest and authentic. Likewise, listening ears translated into caring hearts, and stories about those lost on the bridge cemented relationships.

The simple act of listening not only became good therapy but also acted as a glue in keeping hearts united.

During those first few hours and days following the bridge's collapse, countless individuals walked the talk, and their compassion was exemplary. The strength these individuals displayed in their acts immediately following the tragedy was real. Every word spoken was meant, and every action that followed came from the heart. These were not the words and actions that came from a magazine, a book, or ones prescribed by those at the state or federal level. Instead, all actions came directly from the heart and were motivated by sheer compassion. Individuals mattered because relationships mattered.

And since life is not lived in a vacuum, the display of compassion by local leaders and public figures became contagious in the communities, and a ripple effect began to occur. Dual worship services took place simultaneously on both sides of the river, showing those who had lost loved ones they were not alone in their grief. On both sides of the river, porch lights were not only turned on but stayed on indefinitely as a sign of sympathy and solidarity. Further, corporate acts such as a benefit concert provided financial support for those who lost a loved one on the bridge.

However, the compassion did not stop once the national and international spotlight shifted elsewhere. While attention may have been drawn back to Vietnam, the economy, or national unrest, the caring and compassion on both sides of the river continued unabated. The spotlight on helping to meet the physical, social, and spiritual needs of those in the area continued. This was not a one-and-done effort turned off on December 31 as suddenly as it was turned on December 15. It was a marathon, not a sprint, and acts of caring and compassion went on for weeks and months after the tv cameras, photographers, and newspaper reporters departed.

The heroes in this story are not only those who operated the cranes, divers who worked underwater to recover bodies, or those who risked their own lives to save individuals in the minutes immediately following the collapse. There were countless others behind the scenes who walked the river banks, crewed recovery boats, or headed book drives. Most likely, those in the latter group turned away from public recognition and any kind of community award. In the most accurate definition of benevolence, these individuals acted not out of notoriety but out of love and compassion.

And yet, the deep compassion and sense of remembrance for those forty-six lives lost when the Silver Bridge collapsed did not stop once the Silver Memorial Bridge was dedicated in 1969. A memorial plaque with the names of the deceased and details of tragedy stands at the former entrance to the Silver Bridge in downtown Point Pleasant. A similar memorial stands just north of the former entrance in Kanauga on Ohio Route 7. Both memorials remind travelers that while those that lost their lives on December 15, 1967, may be out of sight, they are not absent from the hearts and minds of those on both sides of the river.

The Conclusion

Just before sunset on December 15, 1967, two small cities, Point Pleasant, West Virginia, and Gallipolis, Ohio, located on opposite ends of a 40-year-old bridge spanning the Ohio River, suddenly became national and international news. Without warning, the 150-year-old relationship between the two cities was temporarily severed because the Silver Bridge collapsed, sending forty-six individuals to their death.

The original design by the J. E. Greiner Company utilized a spun wire suspension system, and the estimated cost to build the bridge was around $825,000. However, the builders of the superstructure, the American Bridge Company, proposed several substitutions to the bridge owners, who promptly accepted the changes because the proposed changes would strengthen the suspension system and cost less to construct the span. The Greiner company had no choice but to go along with the changes.

In place of the conventional use of spun wire cables as the primary suspension system, the bridge utilized heat-treated rolled carbon eyebars. The flat steel eyebars, each nearly 2 inches thick, between 35 and 65 feet in length, and weighing between 2,500 and 5,500 pounds, had drilled eyelets whose diameter measured over two feet at each end of the bar. Placed end to end and joined in pairs of two with vertical hangers between, a giant pin, nearly a foot long and weighing approximately 300 pounds, was then run through the ends of the eyebars, tightened with a large bolt, and capped with a metal plate. Running the entire length of the structure from shore to shore and resembling a bicycle chain, the nearly 150 eyebars stiffened the vertical hangers supporting the trusses and bridge decking.

To support the 700-foot middle span and to further reduce costs, the bridge included a novel way to anchor the eyebar suspension. The construction consisted of driving no less than two hundred 15-foot steel piles into the ground along a 200-foot long, thirty-foot wide trough. Following, the piles were covered with fill dirt to give weight to the anchorage.

A third novelty of the bridge included rocker-type towers.

Here, the 130-foot towers sat on a curved-shaped base constructed atop the two river piers. The rocker-type design allowed some movement in the bridge's deck to compensate for the volume and weight of the vehicles. Additionally, the design permitted some minor movement in response to changes in the tension of the steel cables related to shifting loads on the two-lane, privately-built toll bridge.

From the day of its dedication on May 30, 1928, the bridge served as a shorter route for vehicles traveling between cities in the south and cities to the north and west. Reducing the distance traveled between Charleston, West Virginia, and Columbus, Ohio, by as much as 25 miles, it is believed that more than 4,000 vehicles crossed over the bridge during the first 24 hours it was opened for traffic. Moreover, people on both sides of the river who lived or shopped on the other side of the bridge loved the "connector" since the bridge allowed them to drive directly across the river and not take a slow ferry. Officially called the Point Pleasant Bridge, the bridge quickly took on a new name, the "Silver Bridge," because the bridge was the first in the U.S. to be painted using aluminum paint.

In 1941, the state of West Virginia purchased the bridge from the bridge's owners, the West Virginia-Ohio River Bridge Company (formerly the Gallia County-Ohio River Bridge Company), for $1,000,000. Consequently, the responsibility of inspections, care, and maintenance of the Silver Bridge, and many like it around the state done previously by the private owner, now shifts to the West Virginia State Road Commission. The Greiner Company conducted a full inspection of the bridge in late December. Their recommendations include replacing the bridge's wooden roadway with concrete-filled, steel grid flooring. The state of West Virginia performs a second, full inspection in 1951. The recommendations are to restore disintegrated concrete of the water piers, clean and paint the superstructure, and demolish the toll house. Toll charges remain in place for the Silver Bridge until they are removed on the first day of January 1952. Following established state inspection standards, the Silver

Bridge is inspected in June 1959, January and December 1963, and January 1964. One of the 1963 inspections is performed by a welder and a black top inspector. Following the bridge's inspection in April 1965, nearly $30,000 in recommended repairs are completed. A subsequent report cites no damage. The state conducts two bridge inspections during the first eleven months of 1967 alone and a third on December 6. The maintenance engineer that performs the last inspection reports using binoculars to check the eyebar links and reports nothing of concern. Despite the number of daily vehicles traveling the bridge having increased nearly 40% in the last decade, many believed the bridge to be in good condition, that is, until that cold, late afternoon day in mid-December 1967.

Among the 37 vehicles on the bridge on Friday evening, December 15, 1967, were six on the Ohio approach, 11 on the Ohio span, and 12 on the center or middle span, all heading west. On the opposite side of the bridge and heading east on the center span were eight vehicles, six cars, and two trucks hauling gravel. The vehicles moving west on the bridge included eighteen cars bearing Ohio license plates, five with West Virginia plates, five tractor-trailers bearing North Carolina plates, and one car with Kentucky plates. The vehicles heading east included six cars with West Virginia plates and two with Ohio license plates. The estimated weight of all vehicles at the time was over 485,000 pounds. Among the sixty-four occupants in the thirty-seven vehicles are veterans and retirees, students and teachers, railroad workers and parents, and many other occupations.

Just before sunset, the temperamental stoplight on the far western end of the bridge turns red, bringing traffic headed west to a standstill. The vehicles headed east continued at an average speed. After waiting for what seemed like an excessively long time for the light to turn green, the drivers on the bridge suddenly began to notice that the bridge was shaking more than usual. Unbeknownst to those on the bridge, the inside end section of one of the eyebars immediately west of the 130-foot Ohio tower, later identified as eyebar N330, fractures, causing it to become separated at the joint from the eyebar to its immediate west. Wobbling uncontrollably, the 300-pound pin holding the remaining horizontal and vertical eye bars in that section suddenly pops out, causing the eyebar (C13) to separate from the eyebar to its immediate west (C11). In what seemed like seconds, the whole bridge falls, causing 24 vehicles on the middle and Ohio spans to plunge into the icy waters of the Ohio River. The remaining vehicles either fall on the Ohio shoreline or near the western entrance to the bridge. Immediately, those on the shorelines on each side of the river begin acting.

Two crews from a nearby company located on the West Virginia side of the river jump into their boats and save no less than five people. On the Ohio side, four people are rescued and are taken to Holzer Hospital. Before operations are shut down later that evening, members of the Henderson detachment of the Coast Guard, members of the Huntington District of the Army Corps. of Engineers, the state police on both sides of the Ohio, and local authorities, take their place in the search and recovery process.

Within hours, the Corps. of Engineers closes locks at several dams along the Ohio River between the headwaters of the river in Pittsburgh and the site of the collapse. Additionally, westbound river traffic on the Kanawha River is stopped at the Winfield Locks, all barge traffic for a 35-mile stretch above and below the bridge site is immediately halted from the Racine Locks south and the Gallipolis Dam north until further notice, and an immediate inspection of the Hi Carpenter Bridge upstream in St. Marys is ordered since it was constructed using the same eyebar design as the Silver Bridge. All vehicle traffic into the city of Point Pleasant is immediately halted.

For 17 days, between December 15 and December 31, professional crews and volunteers conduct search and recovery efforts. By the end of the first week, 32 deceased individuals were identified; fifteen were from West Virginia, thirteen were from Ohio, and two were from Virginia and North Carolina. The first of the bodies are recovered on Sunday, December

17th.

As the seventeen days following the collapse progressed, the news surrounding the tragic event seems to fall from the front page of most newspapers. If an article does appear regarding the collapse, it seems almost in the sense of passing or filling extra space. On December 16, the story of the bridge's collapse appeared in sixty articles and no less than one hundred fifty newspapers nationally and internationally. One week later, news surrounding the collapse had decreased to just over sixty newspapers in over twenty states. On December 29, information about the collapse and its aftermath appeared in approximately ten newspapers in eight or so newspapers nationwide. By year's end, if any of the dozen newspapers nationwide are still printing anything about the collapse, it was only a paragraph or two on the last page. Far and above, the most loyal newspapers to stay with the story are the local and regional ones, like the *Athens Messenger* (Ohio), *Charleston Daily Mail*, the *Charleston Gazette*, the *Herald Tribune*, the *Herald Advertiser*, the *Daily Sentinel* (Meigs County, Ohio), and the *Point Pleasant Register*.

With the official exit of the Corps. of Engineers, the Coast Guard, and the West Virginia State Police at midnight on December 31, the state of West Virginia announces it is assuming full responsibility for operations at the site of the fallen bridge. The Corps' final report reads: all but one of the thirty-seven vehicles have been accounted for; thirty-six bodies recovered to date, and ten remain missing. Meanwhile, the last significant portions of the bridge are recovered and taken to Henderson to be reassembled with other parts. The estimated search, recovery, and salvage cost during the past three weeks is over $150,000. The Corps estimates that nearly 1,350 tons of steel are removed from the river, including all of the middle and West Virginia span and parts of the Ohio span.

Several additional bodies were recovered during volunteer dragging operations in January and February 1968. By the start of spring, six more bodies had been recovered and identified, bringing the number of deaths from the Silver Bridge collapse to forty-two. The local authorities increased the number of deceased to forty-four with the recovery of two bodies, one in May and one in June. The bodies of Kathy Byus and Maxine Turner have never been recovered.

Thanks to the efforts of President Lyndon Johnson and a host of other politicians, local leaders receive word that the federal government will pay the entire cost of building a new bridge. The bridge will be located a mile or so south of the old bridge, with one end in Henderson and the other end of the bridge in Gallipolis. As promised, the $14,000,000 bridge was built in less than two years and is dedicated two years to the day of the collapse of the Silver Bridge. The name of the new bridge…the Silver Memorial Bridge…a name chosen to honor those who perished and the symbolic beginning of a new chapter in the life of the two cities.

Just as there is little linkage to those that perished on the Silver Bridge that cold December night over five decades ago, there is no rhyme or reason why some survived, and others didn't. If there exists a correlation, it's of little concern. There was funeral after funeral conducted in Mason and Gallia counties in the weeks following the collapse, eleven in one day alone, December 20. The bridge took away more than forty-six lives that day. It took away the future celebrations and yet-to-be-made memories of birthdays, graduations, and anniversaries. Likewise, the stories of life to be enjoyed and shared with family and friends came to an end on December 15, 1967.

Equally sad, the stories of life that happened during those 17 days seem to have faded over the years. Spouses that lost a mate have remarried and began life anew, and children have grown up and moved away, taking with them the memories. Additionally, those that survived the collapse and those that worked so diligently to restore peace and rebuild lives along both sides of the Ohio are gone, and with them are the first-hand stories of heroism and sacrifice to those in need. As best as can be determined, most of those who survived the collapse have since passed on.

Of the eighteen individuals that were lucky enough to have made it to the western entrance of the bridge on the night of the collapse, only five or so are still alive. No longer able to share their stories of rescue and survival with the world are Gary Meadows, who died in 1989, Howard Rader (1975), Alfred Bingham (1987), Kenneth Remita (2017), W. B. Spann (2005), James Fowler (1985), Betty Fowler (2013), Buddy Fowler (2020), Howard Craig (2021), Walter and Mary Nichols (1985, 1988), and Dewey McCleese (1990). Charlene Woods, who was lucky enough to have stopped at the east entrance of the bridge before it collapsed, passed away in 2010. Who will get the honor of hearing their first-hand story of what it was like in the moments immediately following the collapse?

Likewise, the world will not hear what it was like to risk one's own life to save another or what it was like to suddenly have one's spouse and child suddenly taken away. Those brave souls from the City Ice and Fuel dock that rescued five lives from the icy waters of the Ohio River are gone. Earl Hysell passed away in 2015, as did William J. McCormick (1994), Larry W. McDaniels (2004), Harley Hartley (2005), and Wesley Wears, who lived only five more years after his life-saving act that December night. Wears died in 1972 at the age of 42. George Byus, who not only lost his wife, Hilda but two daughters, Kathy and Kimberly, in the collapse, passed away in 2012. Robert Mayes, who lost his daughter, Darlene, in the collapse, passed away less than three years after his daughter was buried. He was 44 years old. Who gets to sit at the feet of these individuals and hear about their heroic feat or the pain of loss?

And the same stands true for those rescued during those first thirty minutes following the collapse. Those that have passed away include Roadway Express driver Bill Needham who died in 2020, Hennis driver Bill Edmondson (2018), Transcon driver John Fishel (2011), and McLean drivers Frank

Nunn (2019) and Samuel Ellis (2011). Who will get the dignity to hear what they say about the second chance at life they received that night? Granted, their spouses may still be alive, but can they rightfully relate the raw emotions of what it was like to be saved from death?

The same could be stated about the others rescued when the Silver Bridge fell. It won't be river boat captain Howard Boggs because he died in the early days of 2021. As for the other three that survived, no one will hear their story either. The seventh person saved that night, railroad worker, Paul Scott, died in 1997, while survivor Frank Wamsley passed away in 1988. The only female to survive, Margaret Cantrell, died on September 16, 2009. As in the case of the others, they will never be able to answer that heart-wrenching question: why do they think they survived and so many others didn't?

And finally, we won't be able to ask any of those on the front lines during those 17 days that changed America. We won't be able to ascertain what it was like to retrieve bodies that had been submerged for days and take care of the immediate emotional and physical needs of countless people while also getting them to look to the future. It won't be the Civil Defense director on the West Virginia side of the river, John (Andy) Wilson. He passed away in 2000. As for Wilson's counterpart on the Ohio side of the river, John Epling, he died six years later.

Both Epling and his replacement in 1968, Col. W. K. Welker, are buried in Mound Hill Cemetery in Gallipolis. Similarly, we will not be able to know what it was like at the National Guard Armory during those seventeen days when bodies recovered from the bridge's collapse were being brought to the temporary morgue for identification. The Mason County coroner at the time, Dr. Oliver Eschenaur, passed away in 2010. His body was laid to rest in Orrville, Ohio.

Neither will we be able to get a first-hand report of what it was like to coordinate the general search and recovery efforts because the head of the Point Pleasant detachment of the Coast Guard during those seventeen days, Cmdr. Adam Zabinski, passed away in 1992. The person in charge of coordinating the efforts of the Corps. of Engineers, Chief Engineer of the Huntington District, Col. William Falck, passed away in 1982. Likewise, we will not be able to ask Dr. Charles Scheffey. He was not only a member of the NTSB but led a team of investigators that identified the cause of the Silver Bridge collapse as a structural failure. Scheffey passed away in 2014 at the age of 92.

––––––––––––

So who's left to tell the story of the history of the Silver Bridge and how it was built? Who's left to tell about the lives of those forty-six individuals that were lost when the bridge collapsed and how their passing changed the course of bridge safety in America forever? And who's left to tell the story of how cooperation, community, and compassion brought two communities on opposite sides of a bridge together into one epic effort?

––––––––––––

The federal government seems to have done what it could to keep the story alive and pass on the lessons learned by enacting bridge legislation. Prior to 1966, Congress had begun constructing the Federal-Aid Highway bill. As it was initially written, the highway bill would provide funding for the expansion of the nationwide interstate highway system and extend the environmental and legal rights of the federal government to possess private property for public use. However, the collapse of the Silver Bridge caused the federal government to immediately step up its actions in response to the tragedy.

First, within days of the collapse, President Lyndon Johnson appoints a task force to study the bridge's collapse. Headed by the chairman of the newly established Department of Transportation, the task force would look into several areas, including the cause of the collapse and what the federal government could do to expedite the construction of a new bridge. The task force was also directed to work closely with state officials from West Virginia in all areas. Next, President Johnson directs that a national survey be undertaken of all bridges to ascertain their level of safety. Around the same time, Sen. Jennings Randolph, the senior senator from West Virginia, convenes congressional hearings on the collapse.

By April 1968, Congress had amended the Federal-Aid Highway bill to include a section on bridge inspections that mandated bridges longer than 20 feet be inspected at least every two years. Furthermore, the amendment stated that the federal standards be applied to all bridges in the U.S. beyond those built by federal dollars. Upon President Johnson's signature, the bill became law four months later. In the years that followed, additional legislation was passed that included the National Bridge Inspections Standards, which laid-out standards for inspectors and uniform inspection methods. Equally important, the legislation also included the creation of a central database where inspection information could be stored, accessed, and reviewed. As a result, the nation was thrust into a new era of standardized bridge inspections and safety procedures. While the Silver Bridge collapse acted as a wake-up call to the nation and has dramatically changed how the U.S. systematically approaches bridge safety, its efforts came too late to spare those 46 lives.

———————

Likewise, the same could be said of local and regional efforts on both sides of the river, as each has successfully kept the story of the Silver Bridge collapse alive.

At a rest stop located north of the former site of the Silver Bridge on the Ohio side of the river, a plaque was dedicated in 1992. One side of the memorial bears the names of the 46 people who died in the collapse, while the opposite side of the plaque reads:

"On December 15th, 1967, about one mile downstream from this historic marker, a national tragedy occurred. Forty-six interstate travelers lost their lives when the Silver Bridge collapsed into the Ohio River during five o'clock rush hour traffic. The 2,235 foot two-way vehicular bridge connecting Point Pleasant, West Virginia and Kanauga, Ohio via U.S. Route 35. The West Virginia Ohio River Bridge Company built the structure in 1928 for $1.2 million. The bridge, unique in its engineering conception, was the first of its design in America and the second in the world. Instead of woven-wire cable, the bridge was suspended on heat-treated eye-bar (sp.) chains. It was named the 'Silver Bridge' because it was the first in the world to be painted with aluminum paint. In 1969, two years later, its replacement, the Silver Memorial Bridge, was dedicated."

A portion of an actual eyebar is located nearby with a marker that reads:

"This eye-bar (sp.) is similar to the one that fractured causing the collapse of the Silver Bridge on December 15, 1967. The National Transportation Safety Board found that the cause of the bridge collapse was the cleavage fracture in the lower limb of the eye of eye-bar (sp.) 330 at joint C13N of the north eye-bar (sp.) suspension chain in the Ohio side span. The fracture was caused by the development of a critical size flaw over the 40-year of life of the structure as the result of the joint action of stress corrosion and corrosion fatigue."

In 2006, a plaque was erected at the former site of the east entrance to the bridge and reads:

"Constructed in 1928, connected to Point Pleasant and Kanauga, OH. Name credited to aluminum colored paint used. First eye-bar (sp.) suspension bridge of its

type in the US. Rush-hour collapse on 15 December 1967, resulted in 31 vehicles falling into the river, killing 46 and injuring 9. Failed eye-bar (sp.) joint and weld identified as cause. Resulted in Congressional passage of national bridge inspection standards in 1968."

At the foot of the marker sits a simple monument, constructed during the four-year term of Point Pleasant mayor John Musgrave (1977-1980). And nearby, where the West Virginia approach to the bridge used to be, there are 46 brick pavers, each bearing the name of an individual who lost their life in the collapse.

Maybe as early as 2012, the 45th anniversary of the collapse, there has been a yearly observance of the tragedy. The solemn services have traditionally taken place near Main Street in downtown Point Pleasant, the east entrance to the former bridge. In addition to remembrances and a retelling of the bridge's history, the forty-six names of those that passed away when the bridge fell are read, followed by a moment of silence.

On December 15, 2017, the Point Pleasant community recognized the 50th anniversary of the collapse. Beyond words by several federal, state, and local leaders, the somber ceremony included a song written and performed by Steve and Annie Chapman entitled *"The Great Silver Bridge."* A similar observance occurred on the west side of the river in Gallipolis.

In 2018, a mural depicting the bridge was painted on the floodwall at the former east entrance to the Silver Bridge. The painting features a 1928 model vehicle and a 1967 model, representing the years of the bridge's birth and collapse.

At the fifty-second commemoration in 2019, the American Society of Civil Engineers unveiled a plaque at the former entrance to the bridge on the West Virginia side of the river. Recognizing the Silver Bridge as a National Historic Civil Engineering Landmark, it became only the third structure in the state to earn the distinction. One of the other landmarks is the Wheeling Suspension Bridge. The Silver Bridge joins a select list of about 200 or so other landmarks worldwide with such an honor. Among the other notable structures on the prestigious list are the Empire State Building, the Panama Canal, and the Golden Gate Bridge. The bridge plaque reads:

"On December 15, 1967 at 4:58 PM, the 39-year-old Silver Bridge suddenly collapsed into the Ohio River during heavy rush hour and holiday season traffic. Forty-six lives were tragically lost. The cause of the collapse was a single hairline crack in a steel eyebar in the northern suspension chain. In response to this catastrophe, Congress established national bridge inspection standards. These standards created a rigorous nationwide bridge safety inspection program to detect unsafe structural conditions, prevent further tragedies, and save countless lives."

A section of the roadway of the Silver Bridge is entombed beneath the ASCE memorial plaque. Additionally, a similar plaque is expected to be placed on the Ohio side of the river.

In 2017, the *Point Pleasant Register* took home a second-place trophy in the Best Special Section in the annual competition of West Virginia's best newspaper stories. The newspaper's winning story focused on the anniversary of the bridge's collapse. It was entitled "Remembering the Silver Bridge Tragedy, 50 Years Later." Beyond the Point Pleasant paper, the special issue appeared in the December 15 editions of the *Gallipolis Daily Tribune* and the *Daily Sentinel* (Meigs County, Ohio). Ohio Valley Publishing, which owns the three newspapers, also won awards in 2019 and 2020 from the West Virginia Press Association for its special section surrounding remembrances of the bridge's collapse.

In like manner, there have been no less than ten songs written and recorded about the collapse of the Silver Bridge. The list of artists and their songs in no particular order includes two songs by West Virginia native, Ray Anderson (*The Silver Bridge Disaster* and *Why Did It Happen?*), Jim Stout (*Silver*

Bridge History), Little Hot Rod and the Fire Blazers (*Grey Silverbridge* (sp.), and Cecil Pigott's (*The Fate of the Silver Bridge*). Additionally, there is the version by The Three J's (*Silver Bridge Disaster*), the song by Lowell Varney and Jim Horn (*The Silver Bridge*), and two recordings with a similar title, the Barnett Brothers from Cincinnati (*The Great Silver Bridge*) and Charles Alexander and The Carolina Five (*The Great Silver Bridge*). Lastly, one cannot forget the version written by Point Pleasant native, Steve Chapman, and recorded with his wife, Annie, entitled *The Silver Bridge*.

Moreover, at least two books have been written during the last decade detailing the collapse. This includes the 2012 work, *The Silver Bridge Disaster of 1967*, by Stephen G. Bullard, et al., and *The Silver Bridge Tragedy* (Dudding, 2015).

However, the central collection point of much of the history of the Silver Bridge and the retelling of the bridge's collapse has been the Point Pleasant River Museum. For nearly two decades, the museum, under the leadership of the late John Fowler, incorporated the bridge's story into the history of commercial life on the Kanawha and Ohio Rivers. At last report, the museum was the only river museum in West Virginia, and only one of two dozen or so in the U.S. Tragedy struck the museum in July 2018 when fire engulfed much of the 140-year-old building housing the museum. Approximately 60% of the museum's contents are saved, including the 8-foot long and 3-foot high replica of the Silver Bridge that first appeared at the Mason County Fair in August 1968. Plans are underway to rebuild the museum under the name the "Point Pleasant River Museum and Lakin Ray Cook Learning Center."

Finally, this author has done all he could to pass on the history of the Silver Bridge and the aftermath of its collapse by writing this book. In it, I have endeavored to accomplish several things.

First, I've tried to share what I discovered about the lives of those lost on that cold December night in 1967. Those that had their lives ended that day were everyday individuals. They were mothers and fathers, sons and daughters, family members, neighbors, and co-workers. Those 46 lives lost were a true cross-section of America and the Ohio Valley. They included teachers, students, laborers, and honorable veterans. The lives lost that night were innocent lives. They were coming home after working 8 hours or more, going shopping, or transporting goods from one place to another. These individuals just happened to be at the wrong place at the wrong time. I felt it was my duty to share what I learned about their lives before that early winter night in which they passed. Their story before that fatal night needs to be told. Those who survived the collapse by the grace of God can tell their story of being caught by a stop light, being delayed in traffic, stopping by the grocery store, or doing some last-minute Christmas shopping, and by doing so, avoided an untimely death. But I wanted to tell the story of those who did not make it to their destination. I wanted to humanize those twenty-two lives from Ohio, nineteen from West Virginia, three from North Carolina, and two from Virginia as more than a tragic statistic of the deadliest bridge disaster in U.S. history.

In like manner, I wanted to tell the story of those who gave of themselves during those 17 days that changed America. They, too, must have their story told of how they sacrificed and gave of themselves for hours, days, and even weeks in the rescue, search, and recovery efforts. The heroic stories of those on both sides of the Ohio will not be forgotten or their efforts overlooked. These individuals did nothing out of the ordinary. The caring and compassion were not something new to them. It was normal. The fact that nearly everyone on either side of the Silver Bridge knew someone on the bridge that night made not only their efforts more concerted but also an added layer that became a powerful healing tool: love.

Granted, their stories came in bits and pieces, and it was difficult at times to fuse differing accounts of their recollection of events into one narrative. The elements of chaos, confusion, and the passing of over five decades will do that to one's memory. It's expected, and there's no reason for apologies. Truth be told, there were many times I found I had more information than I had room for among the pages. It was then that I came face-to-face with the difficult decision of what to include and what to leave out. Speaking optimistically, what did not find its way into the book provides another author with an excellent starting point for another book on the subject.

But now, their story is out there and in print for the ages. Those that recovered bodies, made and delivered food to workers, and spent countless hours on the river searching for bodies showed the world the depth and degree of their humanity. This work is about a collection of people torn apart by a crack in bridge material the size of two or three sheets of copy paper. But it was about a group of individual lives that were reestablished through cooperation, community, and compassion. As one who was born and raised along the banks of the Ohio River about one hundred miles to the north, I was proud to share their story with the world.

Additionally, I wanted to show that our lives are not, and should never be, lived in a vacuum. Moreover, the world does not stop despite what's happening in our part of the world. The words offered by Ohio Governor Jim Rhodes at the dedication of the Silver Memorial Bridge on December 15, 1969, ring true. "No man is an island," Rhodes is reported to have said, and he's right. There is a whole world beyond what we see and experience daily. There are the cruelties of war, just as there are tragedies connected with mine explosions, flooding, and automobile accidents. But for every tragedy, there are countless acts of caring that show there are good people in this world. Those indefinable numbers of workers that came from all over the U.S. did not have to leave family and friends to assist in search and recovery efforts, but they did. Those who worked the cranes for countless hours recovering vehicles and bodies could have stopped from the stress of the situation, but they refused. Even those who spent Christmas Day eating their dinner aboard a tugboat, students who were searching the banks of the river for countless hours on the weekends, and divers willing to risk life underneath the murky waters of the river, were willing to give of themselves for people they didn't know. Tragedies do that…it brings out the best in people, even though these individuals may wear a hard hat, dress in a uniform, or live in a different county or state. With this work, I am proud to tell their story.

Above all, I wanted to not only show the resolve and spirit of two communities on opposite sides of one of this country's greatest rivers but also how they rebuilt their respective cities, the lives of their citizens, and how their example is one worthy of national attention. At each turn, I endeavored to make the story of the Silver Bridge collapse, the lost lives, and the aftermath not about me.

Throughout, I tried to refrain from offering an opinion on the cause of the collapse, the amount of money awarded to the families of those that lost loved ones, or criticize the way things were done during those 17 days that changed America. I did the same for questions like why the designers failed to consider how certain eyebars, especially inner ones, would be inspected and why only two eyebars were used per section instead of four, as in the case of the Florianopolis Bridge in Brazil. The bridge designers and builders did their best with what they knew at the time regarding materials and construction. There are no photographs among the book's pages that would allow the reader's imagination to intervene. Instead, I allowed the facts gleaned from newspapers, magazines, books, and interviews to lead the narrative.

Despite the presence of unintended irony, including the fact that truck driver and gravel-hauler Alonzo Darst is buried in Gravel Hill Cemetery near Cheshire, Ohio, that Melvin Cantrell most likely performed maintenance on the Silver Bridge, the bridge upon which he died, and one of the companies that sought the contract for ferry service, Point Towing Company, is the same company that employed Marvin Wamsley, my north star throughout the writing of this book has been honesty and truthfulness. Likewise, I learned to work around and through the blatant errors found in some of the sources, like Ronnie Moore was a student at Ohio State University (he was a student at Ohio University), that the Goodyear Plant was in Kanauga, Ohio (it's located in Apple Grove, West Virginia), and that the body of Thomas Cantrell is buried in Mountain Hill Cemetery (his body rests in Mound Hill Cemetery). Anything else would discredit my efforts and heap dishonor on those who lost their lives on December 15, 1967. Ultimately, this story was never about me or what I thought. It's about…

E. Albert Adler, Jr.	Julius Bennett	Leo Blackman
Kristy Boggs	Marjorie Boggs	Kathy Byus
Kimberly Byus	Hilda Byus	Melvin Cantrell
Thomas Cantrell	Donna Casey	Cecil Counts
H. Donald Cremeens	Harold Cundiff	Alonzo Darst
Alma Duff	James Hawkins	Bobby Head
Forrest Higley	Alva Lane	Thomas "Bus" Lee
Gene Mabe	James Maxwell	Darlene Mayes
Gerald McManus	James Meadows	Timothy Meadows
Frederick Miller	Ronnie G. Moore	Nora Nibert
Darius Northup	James Pullen	Leo Sanders
Ronald Sims	Charles Smith	Oma Smith
Maxine Sturgeon	Denzil Taylor	Glenna Taylor
Eugene Towe	Maxine Turner	Victor Turner
Marvin Wamsley	Lillian Wedge	Paul Wedge
James White		

So, can anymore be done to tell the story of the collapse of the Silver Bridge on Friday, December 15, 1967, the 46 lives that were lost, and what happened in Point Pleasant, West Virginia, and Gallipolis, Ohio, in the weeks and months that followed the bridge's collapse? Most definitely. You can tell the story now that you've read this book.

—Dr. Michael F. Price